KINGDOM
CONSCIOUSNESS

A GENERATION'S CALL TO
"COME UP HERE"

VOLUME ONE

MICHAEL GISSIBL

Cover art by Simon Glimm
www.simonglimm.com
Used with permission.

Published by

www.BurkhartBooks.com

Bedford , Texas

Dedication

I dedicate this manuscript to the rising company of disciples that, through a change of mind, will enter the Kingdom realm on earth. May the information contained herein become a catalyst for the formation of Kingdom consciousness in your field of vision. And may the appearance of the expressions of the Kingdom become an inspiration for you to seek first the Kingdom, providing your mind with the information responsible for opening the realm of the Kingdom in your personal experience.

Acknowledgments

I want to thank the Lord Jesus for being such a close companion. Without my daily connection and intimate relationship with Him, my heart would fail. I also would like to thank my wife for her unwavering support throughout the years. The transition from the realm of the carnal mind into the realm of the Kingdom has its challenges. Despite them all, Sheila has always been there encouraging me to journey deeper into the depths of God. For that, I'm grateful to her. I would also like to acknowledge Jack Taylor for the model he's been in my life the past four years. He has inspired me when I wanted to quit, encouraged me when I needed it and built me up when I wasn't expecting it. You have been a companion that, when we have connected, a space has regularly opened in time where the eternal realm has expressed itself in ways it has not while alone. Thank you for being the one who became the one in whom the principle of the synergy of Kingdom consciousness was experienced in my life first. Finally, I want to thank Tim Taylor, founder of Burkhart Books. For two years I labored over this four-volume series on Kingdom consciousness alone. I came to the end of my rope and had no energy or desire to continue. The moment I reunited with Tim, a life came back into me that has energized me once again. Tim Taylor, thank you for being a friend and co-laborer. Thank you for allowing me to experience the substance found in the synergy of "two or more."

Contents

Foreword by Jack Taylor

As you read this book, you will need to keep in mind that the author is a mystic—possibly identified as a "mystic's mystic." Michael Gissibl is my spiritual son. I have watched him from the beginning as he sat for several wordless hours in his first Sons Gathering. He was soaking in the good news of the Kingdom. When he spoke, I knew he was "getting it" and was at once aware that "it was getting him!" He has been "getting it" ever since!

What you are reading in this book is a powerful and pervasive outpouring, as mysterious as it is profound. You will frequently find yourself in stunned disbelief, but read on, reap what you can and, laying aside what is baffling to us non-mystics, allow what resides in your mind to mature. You will find the results to be both intriguing and productive.

You will quickly and repeatedly find that the "Gissibl approach" to truth in general, and Kingdom truth specifically, will challenge cognitive understanding and ignite inner protest. If you, the reader will read on, you will find the uncommon but certain intrigue of the Kingdom of God developing in your thinking. Remember, you are reading the words of a true "mystic."

Now read slowly and carefully and enter the mystery of the ETERNAL KINGDOM!

Jack Taylor,
President, Dimensions Ministries,
Melbourne, Florida

Introduction

There is a door that separates the realm of the carnal mind from the realm of the Kingdom. Jesus is that Door. There is a place on earth opened and available to all, where the non-dual nature of the physical realm and the realm of the Kingdom unify in our conscious experience. Jesus has given us the key to entrance into this field of consciousness—seeking first the Kingdom. Behind this Door lies wonder beyond imagination, beauty yet to be seen with our eyes or imagined with our minds. The added substance in a life realized in the Kingdom realm of consciousness cannot be qualified nor quantified; only experienced. In this Divine domain, there is transformational power reserved for those who've picked up the key of knowledge, which is information of the Kingdom. Authority and influence not seen since the days of old and substance not realized since the days of Jesus await those who enter the realm of Kingdom consciousness. The mysteries of the Kingdom are awaiting those who find themselves in the realm of the Kingdom. There is a remnant of God's people standing at the Door's threshold. Having discovered the key lying in the field of seeking first the Kingdom, we are awaiting the moment the King invites us to unlock the Door. To this point, many have been granted momentary access beyond the realm of the carnal mind. Such pioneers of Kingdom consciousness have tasted of the powers of the age to come with experiences in the "come up here" realm. However, God is preparing groups of disciples, participant's in the divine nature, not to merely experience a taste of the Kingdom but cultivate an abiding presence there. The dawning of the age of the Kingdom-Dwellers is at hand. Those that enter the Kingdom and learn to abide there will become the conduits through which Kingdom attributes are expressed on earth.

> *"Do not call to mind the former things, or ponder things of the past. Behold, I will do something new, now it will spring forth; will you not be aware of it? I will even make a roadway in the wilderness, Rivers in the desert."*
> Isaiah 43:19, NASB

The key to becoming a Kingdom-Dweller is the appearing of the Kingdom in your field of consciousness to the degree it becomes your primary field of vision. Vision experienced first through the eyes of your understanding, then through your physical eyes. The Kingdoms appearance is witnessed only through what Jesus called repentance—a change in your mind. Paul spoke of the result of repentance as the renewing of your mind which is entrance into the realm of the Kingdom experientially. The intent of this book is to provide the reader with material necessary to form the physical substrates of the renewed mind—neuronal correlates of consciousness of the Kingdom. Such material is the key of knowledge which is information of the Kingdom received while seeking first the Kingdom.

Consciousness is subjective experience streamed from one of two fields: the Kingdom field of consciousness or the carnal field of consciousness. The renewed mind provides the screen through which the Kingdom field of consciousness is played out in our subjective experience. The carnal mind provides our subjective experience with a steady stream of consciousness outside the Kingdom field. Seeking first the Kingdom changes the mind by streaming the Kingdom field of consciousness to our subjective experience.

This manuscript was conceived by an experience I had in early 2016 that lasted ten days. I was taken into the Kingdom realm where it became my primary stream of consciousness. During this time, there was no separation in my conscious experience between the physical realm and the realm of the Kingdom.

This non-dual nature formed the basis of my conscious experience. Those ten days enlarged n of life "in the Kingdom" and expanded my vis has in store for His Church in the coming yea does the same for you as I attempt to put int saw, heard, and experienced.

What began as a series of experiences, ended in a un day "abiding journey in the Kingdom." I was no longer having experiences, rather, I was moved into the Kingdom of Heaven on earth and given what I believe was a glimpse of what it will be like walking on earth in the Kingdom in the near future. As our minds are renewed with the information received while seeking first the Kingdom, we are transported into the realm of the Kingdom. As we move into the Kingdom realm, our conscious experience changes. We not only begin seeing things differently, we see different things. The life of the Kingdom and the life in the Kingdom comes alive as the invisible becomes visible. When the Kingdom comes alive to our subjective experience, the evidence of things not seen is realized. We don't see what's in front of us any more than we hear what's been spoken. We see what patterns have been formed in the mind and hear what's been conditioned in the mind by information. In order to "not be conformed by the pattern of this world," we must continually seek first the information of the Kingdom. Then we will find ourselves moving in the direction of conformity to the Kingdom, resulting in practical entrance into the realm of Kingdom consciousness.

The union of the physical realm and the realm of the Kingdom provided me with the capacity to go about my daily life. I was not in a trance or having visions that shut down my ability to be aware of my surroundings; rather, as I was conscious of my immediate environment, present and aware of my surroundings and tasks, I was whisked away in the spirit. I found myself fully aware of being present in the spiritual Kingdom of Heaven and fully present in the physical realm. Every time I was taken in the spirit I was held in superposition, the state of being in two or more places at once. There were several instances when I became aware that I was in four places simultaneously.

en, I was taken to places for the purpose of receiving
ation that needed to be scribed to provide the mind with
tance responsible for growing and developing a renewed
ind. The renewed mind will prove to be the primary conduit
through which the Saints find themselves living in the Kingdom.
Most of this information came in the form of principles or
keys of the Kingdom. This information came primarily from
what I saw and heard and what was downloaded into my spirit.
The "hearing" I'm referring to did not come by way of talking
in a traditional sense but rather through mind reading. In the
Kingdom, as far as my experience went, you communicate with
the Heavenly host through the transmission of thoughts. On
several occasions, information was also presented to me through
smell and taste.

The reason I was privileged with such an extended time in
Kingdom consciousness was twofold; firstly, the Lord wanted to
provide vision for where He's taking His Church. One reason
the Lord does nothing without revealing it first to His prophets
(Amos 3:7) is because He needs to establish a framework of the
mind in order to present conscious experience of His ways on the
earth. In order to lay out a plan, the Lord always finds pioneers
willing to spy out the future. Secondly, I believe my mind had
been renewed to such a degree that this became, in a sense, the
result of a transformed mind. To be transformed by the renewing
of the mind is to be transported into the realm of Kingdom
consciousness. Prior to the time in which I had this experience,
I was seeking first the Kingdom. I had devoted the previous ten
years to making the pursuit of the information of the Kingdom
my top priority. I laid down the pursuit of relationships, money,
and maintaining my reputation as a successful businessman and
church leader to seek first the information of the Kingdom.
For those ten years, I probably averaged forty hours a week
either seeking first the information of the Kingdom or in an
intimate embrace with the Lord, pondering the Kingdom with
Him. During this time, unknown to me, the information of the
Kingdom was changing my mind. This slow and subtle change of
mind brought forth enough of the renewed mind that it began

changing my field of consciousness. I no longer was living by a stream of consciousness from the realm of the carnal mind. Rather, I entered the field of consciousness of the Kingdom and was living out of the realm of the Kingdom. My mind had been conformed with the patterns of the Kingdom to the degree that the Kingdom field of consciousness became my primary field of vision. The more I gave myself over to seeking first the information of the Kingdom the more I experienced states of consciousness in the realm of the Kingdom. In other words, the more the renewed mind grew and developed in me, the more the Kingdom realm appeared to me personally. Beloved, this is our inheritance—entrance into the promised land of Kingdom consciousness.

Renewing the mind, and the means through which the renewed mind grows and develops will be the most important principle discussed in this book. Because the mind is conscious experience, to renew our minds with the information of the Kingdom ensures we enter the field of consciousness of the Kingdom. The neurobiological laws make it impossible to enter the Kingdom without the transformation that only takes place through the renewing of the mind. To be transformed by the renewing of the mind is to be transported into the realm of the Kingdom. To be transported into the realm of the Kingdom is to have your stream of consciousness flowing from the Kingdom realm of Heaven.

"Look! I have set before you today life and prosperity on the one hand, and death and disaster on the other."
Deuteronomy 30:15

There are two worlds in front of us:

1) the carnal world sustained in our stream of consciousness by information taken in from the Tree of the Knowledge of Good and Evil; and

2) the Kingdom of Light brought into our stream of consciousness through the renewed mind which is constructed from the information of the Tree of Life accessed while seeking first the Kingdom.

The two information sources form the patterns that make up our mind which determines the world that appears in our stream of consciousness.

This book is an attempt to extrapolate keys to streaming the Kingdom field of consciousness to your subjective experience. The keys of the Kingdom are designed to transport you into the realm of the Kingdom. The master key, renewing the mind, serves as an anchor by tethering you in the realm of the Kingdom.

There is no way in 50 lifetimes; I could write all I saw during my time in the Kingdom. My future books, God willing, will attempt to put in print the most helpful information in reducing troubles on earth while hastening Heavens reign, both within the individual and on earth. It was made clear to me the amount of suffering and pain inflicted by Satan on the human race during the simultaneous collapse and rise of kingdoms was partly in the hands of the Saints. We have been given more responsibility for culture and government than we presently are aware. I pray multitudes rise up with wisdom to abort much affliction from the dark forces of hell not wishing to relinquish their pseudo position of rulership.

In June of 2013, I was taken in the spirit, and a scroll was rolled out before me. Part of the information in the scroll was an understanding of Isaiah's vision of the temple in Isaiah 6. Perhaps this was the most important piece of information downloaded in me. Each step in the process of the Lord establishing His Kingdom within us contained more information than I could conceive. I desire to present what I believe are the most transformational pieces. In higher heavenly realms, information received "transferred" the form it contained into me, bringing instant enlightenment like a file being downloaded onto a computer. When an assignment was given from this realm, the Spirit of Revelation and Wisdom would take from this "cloud" of information what's needed and download it in the Saint. It was like the "cloud" was in the Saint, and the Spirit of Revelation simply opened a compartment within the "cloud" and brought the information to the Saint's awareness. During my experience, the last three days of documentation I was walking with the Spirit of Wisdom and Revelation and others in the heavenly realm. I saw the Saints that have made it to the Kingdom on earth sharing information until they had all things in common. These overcomers had entered a measure of the "unity of mind" and "unity of faith" responsible for releasing expressions of Kingdom culture on earth. They had become the stream through which the Lord was expressing collective consciousness of His Kingdom onto the earth. As they were entering into Kingdom union, the train of His robe was filling more and more of the temple. The mind of Christ was being formed in the Individual Saint as well as the collective Saints. The death of the carnal man through the cross was also emphasized.

Most of the information in this book I believe to be directional keys for the Church in the coming years. The direction is designed to lead us into the Kingdom experientially, functioning in the "come up here" place that provides us with transformational substance. The "come up here" realm is the field of Kingdom consciousness accessible through repentance—a change of mind. Seeing and having conscious experience of the Kingdom brings freedom beyond our imagination and provides power only granted to those eyes which have become Kingdomized. With this freedom and power comes great responsibility. This responsibility can only be measured once the Kingdom enters one's conscious experience and becomes the predominant field from which one perceives and participates in life.

If you haven't picked up my book "Discovering the Kingdom; a Guide to Seeking First the Kingdom," I recommend you do so. It contains foundational material necessary for the dawning of the Kingdom in your life. Additionally, it provides information responsible for developing the renewed mind. A list of other material to aid you in the forming of the Kingdom mind is in the back of this book. I pray the information in this manuscript brings about a change in your mind to the degree that the "seeing Kingdom realm" opens to you, in order that you might become an active participant in the greatest story ever told: the rediscovery and reestablishment of the Kingdom of Heaven on earth.

Equipping individuals to abide in the realm of the Kingdom is a key to cultural transformation. To transform culture, you must transport culture. To Kingdomize your field of consciousness is the foundation of cultural change. This book provides principles for entering and abiding in the Kingdom experientially by providing the mind with the information responsible for transporting you from the field of consciousness of the carnal mind into the field of consciousness of the Kingdom.

During my ten day experience in the Kingdom realm of consciousness, I was able to scribe about 68,000 words pertaining to the events I witnessed and the ideas spoken to me. After reviewing the contents, I believe "keys of the Kingdom" were presented to me. I received these keys, as best I could, and, for the purposes of this book separated the information into chapter form. The chapters were assembled around specific experiences, a place I was taken, things I was shown or understanding I received. After giving testimony of the specific experience, I presented additional revelation I picked up as I was reading what I scribed of the experience. Additionally, as I began studying material relevant to a specific instance, I gathered further revelation. I've always been a teacher at heart and want to present "digestible" material for you to assimilate. An important part of assimilation is review. In the same way, chewing provides the body with broken down material more effectively taken in, so too does reviewing information provide you with an ability to take in and assimilate the material into who you are. If the goal of truth is to apply it, then reviewing the information provides for such an opportunity. Keep in mind, every time you review a Kingdom truth you are watering a seed. You are providing nutrients necessary for God to bring growth in the realm of His domain.

We are in an age of Kingdom acceleration. This acceleration has a clear, expected pathway. Once you've chosen the Kingdom pathway, there are many diversions from the most direct,

Kingdom life experiencing road. May the Lord bless you for choosing not only the safest and surest path but the path set forth by our Lord Jesus; the path which leads to the field of the Kingdom. This path is none other than the Lord's highest priority for mankind—seeking first the Kingdom.

Preface

FIVE KEYS POINTS FROM MY EXPERIENCE

The five most important points taken from my extended encounter can be seen throughout the book. They are threads woven into the tapestry of my Heavenly experience and are the most important points needing to be emphasized to both the individual and the Church for the coming years. These points are keys needed to equip the overcomers to rule and reign with Christ in the Kingdom realm on earth. They are:

1) Heavens top priority for all followers of Jesus is to commit to the characteristics of a disciple, namely entering the discipline of "seeking first the Kingdom of God." The Disciples chose to make Jesus their teacher. Jesus, in turn, made the disciples His representatives after He transformed them by the renewing of their minds. Heaven's agenda is no different today. Jesus is looking for students to transform into His image and represent His Kingdom. As He does, the realm of the carnal mind, the realm humanity finds itself imprisoned in, will be transformed into the realm of the Kingdom.

The "field" in Matthew 13:44, where the "treasure" was found, is the Field of Kingdomology. Stepping into this field happens the moment we commit to seeking first the Kingdom. Jesus' command to seek first the Kingdom is an invitation to enter the field of Kingdomology. Each moment we receive information of the Kingdom, we are renewing our minds with information responsible for transporting us into the realm of the Kingdom. Walking in this field is demonstrated as we continue seeking the Kingdom above all other fields. As we do, we are sure to discover not only the Kingdom on earth but enter it and begin expressing its character, culture, and influence. When we discover the Kingdom, entering and abiding in the field will become our greatest pursuit. There is a consuming nature of the Kingdom, unlike anything the world has to offer. The more we pursue the field of Kingdomology, the more the Creator of the field pursues us.

2) For those who become established in seeking first the Kingdom, there comes a point where seeking "His righteousness" becomes priority. This transition takes place once our labors in Kingdom-seeking reach a level where we've been conditioned by the information of the Kingdom. The conditioning opens the field of Kingdom consciousness, and we realize that to seek the Kingdom is as natural as breathing. We can't accurately understand righteousness without a revelation of the Kingdom through which our righteousness is connected. Furthermore, once the part of righteousness that addresses our right relationship to the King and His Kingdom is established, the primary objective is preparing us as vessels of influence. Jesus is the savior of the world—the systems of rulership outside His domain. He uses His disciples to establish His influence. Righteousness is the seed which sprouts the fruit of the influence of Heaven on earth through the disciple.

> *"Thy throne, O God, is for ever and ever: a sceptre of righteousness is the sceptre of thy kingdom."*
> Hebrews 1:8

3) For those who make seeking first the Kingdom and seeking first righteousness their number one priority, pursuing the discipline of "only doing what we see the Father doing" (John 5:19) becomes a top priority. This third step only begins when steps one and two have been firmly established within the identity of a disciple. Seeking first the Kingdom of God and His righteousness must become woven into the fabric of who we are. Without such a deep work, it's impossible to enter the discipline of only doing what we see the Father doing. In order to walk in "only doing what we see the Father doing," we must be transported into the realm of Kingdom consciousness. In order to be transported into the realm of Kingdom consciousness, we must be transformed by the renewing of our minds. In order for our minds to be renewed, we must seek first the Kingdom of God and His righteousness.

Author's Note: A disciple committed to seeking first the Kingdom is capable of establishing his identity in seeking first the Kingdom and His righteousness in about two to three years. The condition of the mind prior to entering the "school of Kingdomology" plays a deciding role in how quickly the mind is renewed. There are many whose minds will be renewed much quicker. No matter the time frame, those whose minds are renewed with the information of the Kingdom will become the laborers in the coming harvest (Luke 10).

4) The fourth important emphasis is pursuing the Kingdom within us before being used to take God's authority and establishing it on earth. Jesus needs to establish His throne in us in order for us to effectively represent Him on earth. It is Christ in us that is our hope of influence on earth. It is God that works in us both to Will and to do of His good pleasure (Pilippians 2:13). We must embrace and focus on the work of the Kingdom within us, as a prerequisite to its flowing out from us.

"I have been crucified with Christ, and I no longer live, but Christ lives in me. The life I now live in the body, I live by faith in the Son of God, who loved me and gave himself for me."
Galatians 2:20

5) The fifth point is the acceleration to be expected as we begin embracing the previous "Kingdom concepts," co-laboring with Christ to turn them into our highest priorities. The keys of the Kingdom have been missing for many centuries. The absence of these keys has placed a veil over the "at hand" Kingdom. The reemergence of the Kingdom keys is bringing to life Isaiah 43:18-20:

> *"Do not call to mind the former things, or ponder things of the past. Behold, I will do something new, now it will spring forth; will you not be aware of it? I will even make a roadway in the wilderness, Rivers in the desert. The beasts of the field will glorify Me, The jackals and the ostriches, because I have given waters in the wilderness and rivers in the desert, to give drink to My chosen people ...."*

A necessary key to the advancement of the Kingdom, both within us and on earth, is entering a unity of mind. Community is essential as we grow and develop the Kingdom on earth. The previously mentioned pursuits will only grow and develop an individual so far. The individual must become a living stone, firmly fitted with others. There is an accelerant, a synergy added to a group that is seeking first the Kingdom of God and His righteousness. This accelerant cannot be applied to the individual Kingdom seeker. Authentic community grows out of a group committed to seeking first the Kingdom—a community birthed in the Kingdom, giving expression of the Kingdom on earth.

Jesus taught in groups. He gathered 12 students to Himself and, through the message of the Kingdom formed a unity of mind amongst 11 of them. He never sent out a disciple alone to minister but rather sent them out "two-by-two." Jesus gathered 120 in the upper room where they continued to grow in unity of mind. It could be argued that it was the unity of mind which became the primary spark on the day of Pentecost. Jesus even appeared to a group where He spent 40 days teaching on the Kingdom. All these are examples to us of the importance of cultivating an environment where we collectively begin seeking first the Kingdom. In order for the Kingdom to come on earth as it is in Heaven, we must make room for the Lord to unify our minds with information of the Kingdom. Perhaps implementing schools of Kingdomology will be the most effective way to model the methods of Jesus and bring to pass a measure of unity needed to bring the invisible Kingdom into the visible plane. Until these schools are in operation, may we gather together with a single focus to worship God by seeking first His Kingdom.

ONE FINAL NOTE OF IMPORTANCE

On June 24th, 2013 the heavens opened, and I was caught up in the Spirit. I found myself standing before a time period that spanned 220 years. A scroll opened as time was stretched out and certain events began dropping in me, both past and present. More information was downloaded at that moment than I could quantify. Establishing the Kingdom of Heaven on earth through the cleansing and restoration of the temple—our bodies and mind—was the focal point. Information to help facilitate this process was received. I witnessed many things between 2013 and 2031. The beauty, splendor, and sheer awe of the works of the "Mighty One's," walking in Heaven on earth, captured the attention of the world and its leaders. I saw the Lord's throne established in human bodies (the temple of the Holy Spirit, 1 Corinthians 6:19) and the earth filling up with His influence. In the Kingdom, vision will shatter a present paradigm and implant what is contained in the vision quicker than anything. I pray this book ignites vision for you and implants its content in you.

On January 21st, 2016 I received an email from my spiritual father that seemed to open Heaven, unlocking some of the information downloaded in me in 2013. It seems I entered the timeless, spaceless Kingdom and was lead on multiple journeys to multiple places, mostly being escorted by the spirit of Wisdom or spirit of Revelation. I was carried through time, mostly 2016 through 2026 and was given assignment and direction for the Church and Jesus' disciples. During the experiences, I was writing the encounters as they were happening. I felt I was functioning as a scribe, documenting my experiences as best I could. This extended event began more like an "experience outside of me," in the revelatory realm which I used to perceive as a place outside of me. The last three days were "mind-blowing" as I was given more expansive revelation of the Kingdom within me. Everything in the Kingdom is within us. It is God's greatest desire to first establish His Kingdom within us, before expanding it through us in the earth. This revelation opened the timeless Kingdom inside of me in a way that unveiled a new relationship I now have with the Kingdom and its "living Host." When we enter the Kingdom, we find it necessary to cultivate a new way of communicating. Since the Kingdom is a country, we must learn its language. In order to do so, we must form new vocabulary. A new lexicon of words will prove to be an essential component to repentance: the prerequisite for growing and developing sight within the Kingdom realm of consciousness. The most significant advancements in repentance will come after the schools of Kingdomology are established. Herein lies the key to opening the field of conscious experience of the Kingdom to culture: the persistent study of the Kingdom.

During these ten days, I did my best to document what I saw and the conversations I had. In reading the account, one will encounter new language. Each discovery is a revelation. Revelation, in order for it to serve Kingdom purpose, must not only be received but digested and assimilated into the fabric of who we are. This requires a willingness to revisit the information over and over. Without knowledge morphing into understanding, we are sure to become proud, and pride is a dangerous state of being we all want to avoid.

I pray that you will let faith and patience have their way with you because it's through these two character traits that one inherits the promised Kingdom (Hebrews 12:6). During your journey through this book, I also pray the spirit of Revelation visits you, adding to the appearing of the Lord's marvelous Kingdom in your conscious experience.

This manuscript documents the things I saw, conversations I had, and direction I was given for the Church. A great emphasis was on establishing the "Kingdom within us" and entrusting the King to "move us" into the coming season of expressing the Kingdom on earth. As Christ and His Kingdom within comes to life, the Kingdom will flow out and create visible manifestations for the purpose of cultural transformation. When this happens, it's important we view this as an opportunity to present a new way of thinking by offering the Kingdom as a whole, emphasizing a "Kingdom first" commitment to followers of Jesus.

In the Kingdom, as personal sight is awakened, the "heavenly Host" is availed to us at the Lord's discretion. Like a conductor in a symphony, every living "instrument" in Heaven is under His direction. No movement is made except at the command of the conductor. The domain of Heaven is totally in the hands of the King. In the Kingdom realm of consciousness, one is seated. We are in a posture of rest, waiting to be moved by the King and solely for the King's purposes. As the Saints enter the "manifested Kingdom," they become active participants in the orchestra. In the same way, Jesus did only what He SAW the Father doing; we must receive "Kingdom eyes." This requires us to *"come up here" and "I will show you ... "* (Revelation 4:1). Like with any field of consciousness, the key to entrance into the field is receiving the information within the field. The greater the commitment to the field, the broader one's vision and wider one's influence. For us to become Kingdomized, the Lord must first open our "Kingdom eyes." He does this through the key of knowledge which is reception of specific information carrying unique substance—the substance responsible for growing the renewed mind, which is consciousness of the Kingdom. This substance is held in the information of the Kingdom. It is deposited while seeking first the Kingdom and transformed in the field of consciousness of the Kingdom as we continue seeking the information of the Kingdom. No wonder Jesus rebuked the Pharisees so harshly when He said:

"Woe to you lawyers! For you have taken away the key of knowledge. You did not enter yourselves, and you hindered those who were entering."

Luke 11:52, ESV

Before we go further, I need to expound upon the importance of entering and abiding in the "Kingdom within us."

"In the year that King Uzziah died, I saw the Lord, high and exalted, seated on a throne; and the train of his robe filled the temple ... the whole earth is full of his glory."

Isaiah 6:1, 3b, NIV

I believe Isaiah is describing Saints walking in restored bodies all over the earth and the results of the Lord ruling and reigning in His Kingdom within them. The key phrase is:

"I saw the Lord, high and exalted, seated on a throne; and the train of his robe filled the temple."

When a King went to battle and won, he would go through the enemy's camp and take spoils. The king's greatest recognition was taking a piece of the defeated king's robe and sewing it onto his. The length of the robe would be a visible sign of his greatness. The train of His robe filling the temple is a picture of a Kingdom citizen who's allowed Christ in them to destroy the works of the flesh, bringing greater and greater measures of the divine nature alive and operating in and through them.

As the Lord defeats strongholds and everything contrary to His nature (we call that sin), He takes a piece of that defeated ruler's robe and sews it onto His. Much restoration is needed in the human body. In one particular experience, I saw what I knew to be billions if not trillions of pieces of cloth sewn onto His train. The more pieces covering His robe, the greater the Saint was used in the Kingdom. The sons of God walking the earth were "cleansed by the blood of the Lamb" on a level yet to be understood. When the "train filled the temple," all of creation stopped groaning and acknowledged the manifestation of a son of God. The speed at which this restoration was taking place was not conceivable to the carnal mind. I believe the key to such remarkable transformation is receiving the information of the Kingdom by the steadfast commitment to seeking first the Kingdom. The greater the commitment to seeking first the Kingdom the quicker the transformation.

Author's Note: Jesus is the only man ever to walk the earth with a perfect temple (body). We will never be restored to perfection until we pass into the eternal Kingdom; however, this should not slow our pursuits of "temple restoration." In fact, I pray it propel you to deeper pursuit.

Keep in mind the depth at which the Lord needs to work out of us our carnal nature. It is deep. Each successful triumph in the Kingdom brings to light more carnality.

Be patient and gracious with yourself. There was an initial salvation experience where the Blood of Jesus cleansed you. He gave you His robe of righteousness, and you became a child of the Living God! However, in Kingdom life, there needs to be a practical purity, for no man can stand in the Kingdom presence of the Lord without clean hands and a pure heart. Prepare to be cleansed. Remain humble: quick to confess shortcomings, willing to be placed on the altar of transformation. Resurrection-life begins by "taking up your cross" and culminates at the crucifixion. This cycle needs to be repeated over and over until He returns. Crucifixion makes way for resurrection like your positional righteousness provides a pathway for practical righteousness.

CHAPTER ONE

WHOLE vs. PARTS

A voice spoke, "Come up here." Immediately, I was led away in the spirit. I heard something behind me and turned. The voice beckoned me, "Come, I have something to show you." I looked. Before me was a great kingdom, a massive kingdom. I knew the only kingdom ever to rival this one is the greater eternal Kingdom. After my attention returned to the voice, I heard him say "look," and when I did, I saw the smaller kingdom as a giant pendulum. It was reaching its finality in height. I knew that represented the beginning of its end. The only movement left was in a descending motion. Its downward drop was inevitable and soon to follow. The voice asked me, "Do you know what this kingdom represents?" Before I could respond the answer came to me!

It was the kingdom of the "parts." I knew its fall was caused by the emergence of the information of the Kingdom as a whole being received by sons and daughters of God. I became excited when I realized even the "parts" kingdom was in the whole. This revelation was too deep for me. Its depth overwhelmed me, and I chose not to inquire any further. Then the Lord spoke, "My Kingdom is whole. EVERYTHING is contained in My Kingdom." As He spoke, I saw what He said. This caused my mind to feel like it exploded and I landed beside a river just below Moravian Falls, a waterfall I've visited many times in North Carolina.

I felt the Lord put me there for a reason, but "Why am I scared?" I wondered. "Fear not, the Ancient of days is here," I heard. Suddenly, I knew the fear I was experiencing was not demonic, but holy. I had felt this only one other time, and that was many years ago. I settled down and laid back to enjoy the sound of flowing water. There was an awe-inspiring, captivating silence that took my breath away. I thought, "What's going on here?" It was like everything had stopped. Suddenly, a voice called out from the sky. I thought it said, "Build here for there are scrolls to be opened in the land of printed material." I remembered the Moravians were connected to writing. As I was thinking this, I was interrupted, and a fear came over me.

"Fear not My child. I have reserved this place for some Kingdom scribes. Some of my choicest scribes need to lay down their sword and pick up my law book." Fear once again gripped me, and I said, "Lord, I don't want to know anymore." He pushed back and in a confident tone responded, "Your back will always hurt from carrying weight I never called for you to carry. Don't entertain thoughts outside My will." I bowed in agreement and found myself back at Moravian Falls, connecting with the beauty of the flow of water.

A voice spoke to me, "Specific manna from Heaven will fall here in the near future. Prepare My people." I felt 2017 and 2018 were the time periods in which this revelation would fall. The moment I thought that my head shook like it was in a paint shaker. "You are trying to discern what I haven't given you permission to see. Don't try to discern, obey." I heard a voice thunder the word "PRAY!" As I departed from this place, I felt I would revisit it again at another time. A dove landed on my shoulder and directed my attention to the mountain peaks I saw earlier and said, "Remember the season you are in. Scatter the 'seek first the Kingdom' seed, open the door to the whole, and provoke the people to leave the parts."

Key to the Coming Kingdom Reformation

In June of 2017, I spent a weekend in Moravian Falls at a prayer gathering. I believe, at least in part, the Lord fulfilled the prophecy, "Specific manna from Heaven will fall here in the near future. Prepare my people," while I was there. The following is a revelation I received and subsequently shared with a group of praying Saints at Moravian Falls. My stated intent in sharing the revelation was to sow a seed into the soil of Moravian Falls that would sprout a Kingdom reformation, resulting in the spread of a nationwide revival. The following is a rendering of what I received and subsequently shared. Paul said,

> *"But when that which is perfect comes, then that which is in part shall be done away."*
>
> 1 Corinthians 13:10, KJV

This principle has profound implications regarding the Kingdom and its accelerated expression, both within the believer and on earth. The Holy Spirit, through Paul, is saying to the individual, "When the whole becomes your primary field of consciousness, the parts will no longer be paid attention to." The parts will vanish from your conscious experience. They will be done away with because the opening of the field of the Kingdom will be the new pattern expressed by the renewed mind. Being conformed to the pattern of this world will be done away with. The kingdom of the parts, which once dominated your awareness, will be done away with. Why? Because the lens of the field of the Kingdom will be formed with the sufficiency required to see into a new world. The parts become swallowed up in the whole and you are given eyes to see the whole, even in the parts. When this starts, the invisible becomes visible, and the visible begins disappearing. In the same way the god of this world blinded humanity from conscious experience of the Kingdom by taking away the information of the whole, so too will the Lord blind humanity from the kingdom of darkness by taking away the information of the parts.

This "Kingdom law," as stated in 1 Corinthians 13:10, not only affects the individual but nations as well. The key to the "whole" affecting nations hinges on groups of individuals coming together with the unity of the renewed mind formed through the collective, steady, taking in of the information of the whole. Jesus called this group His Church, and He called the individuals His disciples. The synergy created by two or more disciples assembled with their consciousness in the Kingdom sparks an accelerant that expresses the substance of Heaven on earth. Ultimately, the culture made manifest through the carnal mind is exchanged for the culture of the Kingdom being expressed through the renewed mind. The more people assembled with renewed minds, the greater the impact of the Kingdom's expression.

As Saints arise with renewed minds patterned after the information of the whole, a major shift will transpire. Entrance into the Kingdom will take place experientially, allowing for a new dwelling place in the realm of the domain of God. This will change everything. No longer will the Lord need to come down to work with man in his carnal domain, but rather man will begin working with God in His.

At present, the Lord has been working with man's Church which is rooted in the realm of the carnal mind, doing all He can to draw us up into His atmosphere of reality. Due to this relationship dynamic being rooted in the carnal, fleshly realm, the Lords operations in and through us are limited. Despite His attempts to draw us up into His realm, the Church has remained carnal and of the world, blind to the means of ascension. However, when the Lord sees His Kingdom model rising in the minds and hearts of His sons and daughters, His primary attention shifts from trying to work with man, to devoting His time to those who have begun working with Him. Beloved, there are men and women in whom the Lord has found carrying His Kingdom model on earth, and many more will rise up in the coming years. Their minds are being renewed with the information of the whole, causing them to be transported up to the higher realm of existence—the realm of the "come up here." This domain is where the higher life of working with God is experienced and expressed through the renewed mind which is consciousness of the Kingdom. In this realm, the outworkings of the Kingdom and the preaching of the Gospel of the Kingdom become the predominant activity leading to cultural transformation. Therefore, we must conclude that all our efforts of trying to express the Kingdom through the pursuit of signs, wonders, healings, evangelism, salvation, and all other parts of the Kingdom, have not worked. We must make a concerted effort to leave behind the pursuit of the attributes of the Kingdom in favor of giving ourselves over to seeking first the whole.

The key to ascension into the Kingdom realm has been taken from the Church but is being restored in our generation. This Treasure has always been hidden in the field of study of the Kingdom, present and available to all who enter. Religion has taken away the field of the Kingdom by presenting us with the field of theology. Theology has formed man's Church the same way Kingdomology will form Jesus' Church through the formation of conscious experience by way of information of the Kingdom. Religion has replaced Jesus' greatest command to seek first the field of Kingdomology and substituted it with the field of theology. This one "sleight of hand" has taken away the key of knowledge which is information of the Kingdom. This diabolical plan began all the way back in Jesus' day, as evidenced in His rebuke:

> *"Woe to you experts in the law because you have taken away the key to knowledge. You yourselves have not entered* [the Kingdom], *and you have hindered those who were entering."*
> Luke 11:52, NIV

How did they do this? By taking away the "key to knowledge" which is receiving information of the whole, which is information of the Kingdom.

Satan has worked so tirelessly to keep the information of the Kingdom from us because sight of the Kingdom is received the moment the parts are done away with. Doing away with the parts by receiving information of the whole, sets in motion the biological actions required to form the renewed mind responsible for taking us into the realm of consciousness of the Kingdom. In order to take in the whole, we must seek first the information of the Kingdom. The only way to begin this process is entering the field of Kingdomology, which is seeking first the information of the whole. This means of transformation actualizes the mandate to "come up here" and provides the Church with substance capable of fulfilling the Will of God on earth as it is in Heaven. The only way the parts are done away with is by receiving information of the whole in greater measure than receiving information of the parts. This specific protocol sets the stage for transportation from the realm of the carnal mind into the realm of the Kingdom by collapsing the mind patterns of this world and structuring the mind patterns that result in Kingdom consciousness. To be transformed by the renewing of the mind is to be translated from the realm of the carnal mind into the realm of the Kingdom experientially. This is an essential key to overcomers stepping into their identity as co-laborers, ruling and reigning with Christ on the earth (see Revelation 3:21).

Before the realm of the parts were done away with, revelation was a momentary slip into the realm of the Kingdom. It was Heaven visiting the carnal realm on man's terms. When the realm of the whole comes, revelation takes on a new form. The added substance transforms a revelatory experience into an abiding spirit that is awakened in one's consciousness. Revelation of this nature is found, according to Ephesians 1:17 in specific knowledge. This knowledge is referred to as the "knowledge of Him," which is information of the whole—the Kingdom. Now, revelation becomes a facet of the eternal realm gifted and opened to us. This distinction reflects a life lived out of the carnal mind versus a life lived out of the renewed mind of Christ.

Jesus brought an end to that which is in part. He provided His disciples with the whole by presenting the information of the Kingdom. As we seek first the Kingdom, we form neuronal communities in the brain responsible for consciousness of the Kingdom. At the same time, we are putting to flight the assembled neurons responsible for the realm of the carnal mind expressing itself in our field of consciousness. As long as we continue to seek first the Kingdom, we ensure the scattering of the neurons responsible for the carnal mind. Eventually, the subsystem of the carnal mind that is scattering will be put to flight and cease to exist, causing it to lose its ability to generate conscious experience of the realm of the carnal world.

We cannot analyze or experience the whole through the parts. In the Kingdom, the parts have no independent existence. The Church has been divided into separate parts. This has been the primary cause of Her weakened state and inability to bear lasting fruit in keeping with the Kingdom. In this emerging age of the Kingdom, as we inherit conscious experience of the Kingdom, we come under a new set of laws and standards, releasing a very different result. The kind of results we witness in the life of Jesus, His disciples, and the Book of Acts. The message will be similar, just not expressed from the position of understanding it apart from the whole. The missing ingredient which distinguishes the part from the whole is the very ingredient that will take the lifeless Church and thrust Her into expressions of the eternal Kingdom. By and large, the message of the Kingdom of Heaven has been fragmented and dispersed throughout the collective Body of Christ. As members of the Church discover the Kingdom, they will gather the "parts" and discover the information was created in the "whole" and that it was man who fragmented it into parts. This catastrophe formed the carnal mind which brought consciousness of another kingdom—the kingdom of ignorance.

"God did extraordinary miracles through Paul, so that even handkerchiefs and aprons that had touched him were taken to the sick, and their illnesses were cured and the evil spirits left them. Some Jews who went around driving out evil spirits tried to invoke the name of the Lord Jesus over those who were demon-possessed. They would say, 'In the name of the Jesus whom Paul preaches, I command you to come out.' Seven sons of Sceva, a Jewish chief priest, were doing this. One day the evil spirit answered them, 'Jesus I know, and Paul I know about, but who are you?' Then the man who had the evil spirit jumped on them and overpowered them all. He gave them such a beating that they ran out of the house naked and bleeding."

Acts 19:11-16, NIV

Here is an example of Paul, a man ministering from the perspective of the "whole" and others out of the "part." Witchcraft and sorcery often become the expressions of those attempting to perform in the flesh what can only be brought into existence in the Spirit.

Mark 3:24 (NIV) reads:

"If a kingdom is divided against itself, that kingdom cannot stand."

The Greek word "divided" means: divide into parts. Satan has divided God's Kingdom into parts and has no problem with us as long as we don't discover the whole. We can talk about Jesus all we want and even prophecy in His name. As long as we don't discover the only means by which Satan's kingdom collapses, all is well in his world. Satan knows, to receive parts of the Kingdom is to receive none of it. However, once the whole is discovered, Satan's governance on earth begins its descent into eventual nothingness. Every time we study the parts, we are participating in the partitioning of God's Kingdom, maintaining and enforcing its collapsed state within our field of consciousness. We also become unknowing participant's in concealing its existence by hindering its outward expression. As soon as we receive a revelation of the whole and begin receiving information of the whole from the place of the whole, God's Kingdom is put in a position where it stands and Satan's collapses.

To you personally, this opens a new source of life which carries and expresses additional substance; collectively, it establishes cultural and social change. The greatest need of the hour is a revelation of the whole which will be brought to your awareness as you seek and continue seeking the Kingdom. Don't give up! You are one revelation away from personally experiencing Heaven on earth! This experience carries with it such a strong pull that it's sure to leave you wanting more. Knowing the root cause of your experience— seeking first the Kingdom—will drive you deeper in obedience to Jesus' highest priority for you- seeking first His Kingdom.

If I divide up a shirt into parts, it ceases to become a shirt. It no longer has the ability to function in its designed purpose. No matter how much I try to see a part of the shirt as the shirt, I can't. It must be presented as the whole for it to be seen as it was intended and for it to serve the manufacturer's purpose.

Koinonia is the scriptural word for Kingdom fellowship. This word informs us of a spiritual fellowship found in Kingdom living. In a message he shared at Moravian Falls, North Carolina on January 31, 2016, Rick Joyner said,

> "Koinonia is being bonded together to such a degree you can't separate the parts without them dying."

This is a good example of what happens every time we divorce a part of the Kingdom from the Kingdom. We will still produce a manifestation of the part, but the attributes of its origin, Heaven, are missing. In a practical sense, when we fragment a part of the Kingdom, we kill the substance which makes up the essence of what we are wanting to present. In order to resurrect the essence of the Kingdom, we must lay down our pursuits of the parts of the Kingdom and seek the Kingdom as a whole.

CHAPTER TWO

RESTORING THE TEMPLE

Preparing to Carry
the Glory and Splendor of God

"You have heard these things; look at them all. Will you not admit them? From now on I will tell you of new things, of hidden things unknown to you. They are created now, and not long ago; you have not heard of them before today, so you cannot say, 'Yes, I knew of them.' You have neither heard nor understood; from of old your ears have not been open."

Isaiah 48:6-8a, NIV

"The days are near when every vision will be fulfilled. For there will be no more false visions or flattering divinations among the people of Israel. But I the Lord will speak what I will, and it shall be fulfilled without delay. For in your days, you rebellious people, I will fulfill whatever I say, declares the Sovereign Lord. The word of the Lord came to me: Son of man, the Israelites are saying, 'The vision he sees is for many years from now, and he prophesies about the distant future.' Therefore say to them, 'This is what the Sovereign Lord says: None of my words will be delayed any longer; whatever I say will be fulfilled, declares the Sovereign Lord.'"

Ezekiel 12:23b-28, NIV

I was taken to a place where I saw the Lord high and lifted up. He was sitting on a throne the size of a city block.

I remembered Isaiah 6 and wondered, "Where is His train?" I heard the Lord say, "If you knew where you are you would not concern yourself with My train." Immediately I could see I was inside a human being. Then He said to me, "My train will fill this temple as awareness of My Kingdom is awakened." Suddenly bread appeared with waves in it, and I heard, "This is bread from Heaven." I thought, "Is this the bread of His presence?" I heard, "This is not for you to know now. Know this; I am sitting on the throne of many hearts waiting for them to pick up the key to filling My train in our temple." I thought, "What a God that He would share His throne with man." My attention was seized and brought back to the Lord when He said, "Don't get distracted. Stay on the task at hand." I knew Him to mean spreading the mandate to seek first the Kingdom of God and His righteousness with the emphasis on seeking first the Kingdom.

I sensed this is the primary mandate for the Church, a mandate that will lead us into the realm of the Kingdom—the field of Kingdom consciousness. I felt that we would forever be active in this mandate, but assignments would be added. I believe revelation of His righteousness imputed to us would be added once seeking first the Kingdom was firmly rooted. I heard a voice respond, "You are correct but dangerously close to falling." I thought, "Pride comes before a fall," and fearfully agreed in godly sorrow.

I took a deep breath and returned to His throne where I laid at His feet. A while later, I saw my mind fly away on what looked like a magic carpet and heard a voice say, "It takes intentional focus to remain engaged on the task of seeking first the Kingdom. I will remove the enticement of the magic carpet if you will make an effort to lay down the things of the world in exchange for seeking My Kingdom." As He was speaking, I felt such compassion and grace that the slightest move towards this end would begin the removal of the option of the magic carpet. Just as I thought this a window appeared to my left and something moved passed it that was dark, and I heard a voice say "In all dimensions of Kingdom living on earth, there is the temptation to be distracted." It was then that I realized I was being moved to another dimension.

"Up here your assignment is to stay focused on only doing what you see Me doing." I thought, "What about seeking first the Kingdom." He responded, "Up here, Kingdom first moves into your identity. It becomes part of your nature." When He said this, I saw a brain where seeking first was resting but fully awake. It moved into multiple places at once until it was everywhere all the time. I thought, "This is amazing!" While pondering this Kingdom dynamic, I wondered, "Could it be, the discipline of seeking first the Kingdom rewards you with a conditioning of the mind that moves you into the field of consciousness of the Kingdom?" Could it be that the information of the Kingdom, received while seeking the Kingdom, re-patterns the brain so that it generates a state of being within the field of the Kingdom, expressing the perpetual perception of the Kingdom? Could it be that seeking first the Kingdom is part of our eternal state of being?" At that moment, my emotions became conflicted. I was overwhelmed at the beauty of Kingdom life while grieved at how far we have fallen as a human race. My thoughts drifted: "If only we could raise up a generation whose highest intent was to step into their eternal calling of seeking first the Kingdom."

Then a voice from a large group worshiping in Heaven spoke, "I am giving those in this dimension the lost sheep of the house of Israel. They will be your field of treasure." I knew the "lost sheep" to be those disciples of Jesus possessing the attributes of a disciple with the exception of seeking first the Kingdom and becoming a teacher of the Kingdom. I knew the earth would be opened up to receive the Kingdom in an accelerated manner once these "lost sheep come home." The Lord spoke, "I have gathered them. Go get them." I knew where they were, but the command seemed impossible. It was then I remembered the power of prayer. I prayed, "Oh Lord, raise up a remnant to introduce the lost sheep to the discipline of seeking first the Kingdom so that they might enter their destiny as disciples, teaching the message of the gospel of the Kingdom, and transforming hearts, cities, and nations for the Kingdom. Oh Lord, raise up the leaders in whom these lost sheep follow. Raise them up to become the conduit's through which the information of the Kingdom flows into the hearts and minds of the lost sheep, growing and developing the field of consciousness of the Kingdom." I stood in the silence and could hear movement in the Heavens. Faintly, I could see what looked like angelic hosts preparing to act on my prayer. They were moving in a hasty but graceful manner. I knew they weren't anxious, but clearly excited to begin fulfilling the prayers.

I was then lifted into a vision where I saw a boy sleeping. He was awakened and before him was a box. Coming out of the box was darkness. This darkness entered his ears and eyes and began eating him. I thought, "How can this be?" A voice spoke through the worship I knew to be coming from the throne room and said, "You are being made the temple of the living God. There can be no mixture. Do away with all that breathes a breath from hell." The boy agreed, got out of bed, and the vision ended.

I asked the Lord for greater meaning and heard worship at the throne becoming louder and more intense. A voice spoke, "Saints in the Kingdom, those who reach this level of temple restoration can no longer entertain things of this world." I thought, "Oh how I wish all believers could enter this level." I heard the voice respond, "That is none of your business. Keep focused on 'only doing what the Father is doing.'" I became worried. Fear of failure and loss began awakening emotions in me I knew originated from my carnal man. My spiritual man responded in a loud shout, "Take this away my Holy God. I want to be conformed to Your image." Immediately, just before I finished crying out, I felt the Lord drawing me closer to Him as I followed.

Greater awareness of where I was came to me. "I'm really in the Kingdom of Heaven on earth," I thought. Suddenly, I saw Satan fall like lightning, and a voice spoke, "You are indeed here. You will become more aware the longer you remain in the Kingdom within. Only let this be a reminder, you are as easily capable of falling like lightning." I swallowed, and a gulp hit my throat as I thought, "Oh God help me." A picture of Holy Spirit smiling came to me and I became aware that the voice traveling with me on this journey was often Holy Spirit. I sighed in confident relief and journeyed on.

I found myself walking on a path. In my right hand was a torch with a flame. I remembered, "Your word is a lamp to my feet and a light to my path." When I thought this, a light off in the distance blinded me. It was so far away; I couldn't calculate the distance. I knew the light to be the light coming from the presence of the Father sitting on His throne. I heard a voice, "You hold a piece of that light always. It will guide you to your destination on earth." When he said this, I was taken inside the Isaiah 6:1-body. I saw it was growing and multiplying; getting bigger and bigger and covering the earth. I heard a voice from the throne say, "Get rid of all filthiness and abide in the light." I felt that statement was primarily directed to the renewing of the mind which involved the collapsing of the carnal mind through the receiving of the information responsible for growing the renewed mind. That information being the information received while seeking first the Kingdom.

My attention turned to the multitudes on my left. They were involved in all manner of foolishness such as unwholesome entertainment, riotous living, perverse talk, and all things outside the Kingdom. I even saw things that had the appearance of being admirable such as seeking first specific attributes of the Kingdom. Many were talking to each other, but it was idle talk —talk that amounted to nothing. I realized even "good" is bad when you become Kingdomized with a Kingdom perspective. I thought, "We have to plant the 'whole' seed not the 'part' seed." I could see that all "good" activity was rooted in the carnal mind and were the seeds of the "parts." I also knew that the collapsing of the carnal mind and the simultaneous emergence of the renewed mind begins with seeds of the "whole" being planted.

My right ear suddenly tickled. As I began scratching it, a voice spoke, "You have entered the better way of Kingdom life. You can no longer carry with you contamination." When he said this, I saw a river flowing with crystal clear water. I thought, "Is this the next step? Am I being prepared for the river?" I left this place and found myself in a classroom. I was sitting at a desk, and a book opened before me. There was worship in this room. They were singing about "the better way." When I looked at the book, it opened and on the left page was written "Eden Restored" and on the right read:

"Then the angel showed me the river of the water of life, as clear as crystal, flowing from the throne of God and of the Lamb, down the middle of the great street of the city. On each side of the river stood the tree of life, bearing twelve crops of fruit, yielding its fruit every month. And the leaves of the tree are for the healing of the nations. No longer will there be any curse. The throne of God and the Lamb will be in the city, and his servants will serve him. They will see his face, and his name will be on their foreheads. There will be no more night. They will not need the light of a lamp or the light of the sun, for the Lord God will give them light. And they will reign forever and ever."

I knew this was Holy Scripture. A man stood up and read it. As he did, meaning and content began leaving the page. I thought, "This truly is alive." I heard a voice, "Stay focused." My attention went back to the life coming from the Holy Word of God. I heard the voice, "Seal up what you have seen until the torch is taken from your right hand. I thought, "How will I know when that takes place?" The voice, which I now knew was the Spirit of Wisdom, spoke, "I am with you. Let the vision I have opened to you be an encouragement," when she said this; I realized we were in the Isaiah 6:1-body.

I read this twice as the living word resurrected. "Seal its contents. Only share Eden within," Wisdom declared. I knew she was wanting the Saints to know that Eden restored is within the believer first. I was reminded, as I entered the throne, to seek first the Kingdom within. I fell on my face in astonishment. I thought, "Eternity, Oh God, you have put in our hearts. May you raise up a group that discovers Your Kingdom within."

I heard the words, "'Hear, Oh Lord, I have prepared a resting place for you' being sung by a large group." This encouraged me until I realized the Spirit of Wisdom was no longer with me. I became fearful, and the group got louder and more intense. "Hear, Oh Lord, we are ready. We have prepared a home for you" they sang. It was beautiful. As they were singing, I saw the cleansing of the temple taken to another level.

It was then I realized with greater understanding, it's all about the Kingdom within. We are only to pursue the Kingdom within, leaving the Kingdom on earth to the Lord. "You are correct son. No man is ready to express and establish My Kingdom on earth, yet." Another voice jumped in, "We must establish the throne in the micro before the macro." When He said this, understanding appeared in me, and it made sense. First, the Kingdom in the individual, then movement outward, culminating in the earth being filled with the King and His domain.

Suddenly, awareness of Heaven expanded, and I saw things I was told to seal up for now. Peace fell on me. Out of the peace, the Spirit spoke, "Tell the Saints to pursue the Kingdom within. These are those who I will use to blow the wind of My Spirit over the earth."

Suddenly, a wind took me back to a place I knew. The Lord spoke, "Wait for me alone. You have seen what things outside My Kingdom do to the Isaiah 6:1-body. I will bring others to you of like mind. They will help keep your focus on My Kingdom within." When He said this, I was lifted in a transportation vehicle flying faster than what I knew to be the speed of light. As we were traveling, I saw in the atmosphere the Word-community.

That's when information from within the word was downloaded in me showing how and why and what community will look like in the future.

"These things I have spoken to you while abiding with you. But the Helper, the Holy Spirit, whom the Father will send in My name, He will teach you all things, and bring to your remembrance all that I said to you."
John 14:25-26, NASB

Then I realized, in order to actualize what I was seeing in the future, I had to go back to the past. When I thought this, I was taken to a period of time during the book of Acts where the Lord was standing.

What I had just seen caused me to ask, "But Lord how is anyone going to listen to me? Society is so far from embracing what you are showing me." When I thought about this, I realized I was wrong. Visions of places in America flashed before my eyes, and I understood that God has been preparing for this behind the scenes. Oh my goodness! Now I knew in a broader measure just how big His beautiful Kingdom is! He responded, "Keep your mind on the task at hand. I will do My job. Let Me take care of what I take care of and remember you are in the realm of 'pursuing only what you see the Father doing.'" A wind blew me away, and I found myself before the throne, energized with passion and commitment.

In a vision, I saw the Lord taking "parts" of the Kingdom found in the earthly Church and redeeming them by adding the substance only found in the whole. I saw Him placing the parts of the Kingdom, which were now made whole, in the restored temples (bodies of the Saints), and using the attributes to influence the earth. I watched those activated in the gift of prophecy in the earthly Church become prophecy in the Kingdom Church. I saw a group in the earthly Church receiving revelation, and a group in the Kingdom Church become alive with the Spirit of Revelation as they moved in and through the realm of the Kingdom while on earth. It appeared they may have been standing on earth, in Heaven, with their spirits being escorted, directed, and moved into the realm of the Kingdom, then brought back into their bodies.

All activity was done within. I realized how important it is to understand several quantum concepts in order to grasp existence within a place where there is no time and space. I understood that the pursuit of the parts resulted in the form contained in the parts, while the pursuit of the whole contained and expressed the form within the whole. As understanding came to me, I was able to experience both realities. Then suddenly, the Lord shifted me out of both realities into the Kingdom only. When this occurred, I saw with greater clarity how much more impactful the Kingdom way had been. I also became aware of how the pursuit of the "parts" was a tool in the enemy's toolbox used in his "divide and conquer" strategy. I realized in greater measure how important it is for the Saints to receive a revelation of the Kingdom as "whole." The importance of entering the field of the Kingdom through seeking first the Kingdom became more apparent to me as I realized a key to the appearance of the substance only found in the whole was entering and abiding in the field of the Kingdom.

Author's Note: It is my estimation that these individuals have begun to arise in efficacious numbers in 2016 and this group will continue to grow in size. The fruit from this realm of living will cause the Father to move us into the next phase of Kingdom consciousness. There will be a subsequent season of growth in the Kingdom on earth, followed by such Kingdom awareness that the collective consciousness and perception of many will be moved into the non-dual nature of the physical and spiritual realm. For such is the place of the emerging Kingdom-dwellers.

Times are tough and will only get tougher in the world governed by the carnal mind. It is my belief that God's most pressing assignment to ready Kingdom-dwellers for harvest time is seeking first the Kingdom of God and His righteousness. During this time, the Church will be placed on a fast track from transition as an earthly organization run by man, to a Kingdom Church being built under the leadership and construction of Christ in the realm of the come up here.

When "revival" breaks out, the key to ensuring one is in the Lord's House rather than one built by the end time false apostles and prophets is the subject of teaching the Kingdom and the character of leadership. The enemy will be working hard in the areas of "revival" where the leadership is not dead to their own fleshly, carnal nature. Emotionalism and hype in leadership open the door to spirits of darkness. Where the message of the gospel of the Kingdom is being preached in humility and brokenness, Jesus will be building His Church. Where the message of the parts of the Kingdom is being preached with hype, emotionalism, and self-centeredness, the kingdom of darkness disguised as an angel of light will dominate.

I witnessed Kingdom citizens who had no carnal emotions left in their bodies as they died daily to them—no worry, no fear, no shame, no guilt, no unholy emotions. The revelation of the Kingdom had reached a depth culminating in such transformation that fleshly emotions ceased. I could see a narrow way, and like a funnel, people were being led down that path. At the end was a door and written above it were the words "seeking first the Kingdom." An angel guarding the door stood and with his eyes scanned the hearts of those wishing to enter. I knew he was looking for a specific character trait within the heart. That trait is the degree to which the heart intends to seek first the Kingdom. All those with the intent to seek first the Kingdom entered the Kingdom realm of consciousness in due time.

There was a school with desks and many, many teachers. All the teachers had on their foreheads "seeking first the Kingdom."

I looked at the students foreheads and growing out of it were the words "understanding the Kingdom." Every student was understanding at different levels as evidenced by how complete the phrase "understanding the Kingdom" was written. When they reached a certain level, a bell rang, and the teacher stamped on their foreheads "seeking first the Kingdom." They gave them a manual titled "Holy Spirit" and sent them to teach.

I was then taken to another room that was not so cheerful. As I entered the room, I looked and saw the appetite for the flesh in the people being starved and a divine appetite nourishing the students who I knew were of a royal Family- the Family of God. I saw the distribution of nourishment I knew was fulfilling Jesus' words: "I have food you know not of." I became aware of the ability within the Saints to ascend and descend dimensions. Flashing lights in the sky with the words fasting, stillness, sacrifice, and suffering were indicating ascension-vehicles. I knew practicing these disciplines would move an individual closer in proximity to the Father.

In one instance, I moved so close to the Father that I thought I might die. I felt I needed to make a decision. Do I "give up the ghost" and enter the eternal Kingdom or do I conclude as Paul, "For me to live is Christ and to die is gain." Knowing much work needed to be done, I chose to live.

"See, I will send my messenger, who will prepare the way before me. Then suddenly the Lord you are seeking will come to his temple; the messenger of the covenant, whom you desire, will come,' says the LORD Almighty. But who can endure the day of his coming? Who can stand when he appears? For he will be like a refiner's fire or a launderer's soap. He will sit as a refiner and purifier of silver; he will purify the Levites and refine them like gold and silver. Then the LORD will have men who will bring offerings in righteousness."
Malachi 3:1-3, NIV

SUPERFOODS: Restoring the Temple

I took a bite of something that tasted like cabbage. It was a large bite. So big in fact, I could hardly chew. When I swallowed, I could see millions of military soldiers sent to destroy what I knew to be robbers in the temple. I was led away to a place called Restoration where I heard a teacher speaking. As I approached him, he hurled something that looked like a ball covered in gold or a ball of gold. It flew in me, and he said, "Here's some content relating to restoring My temple. Take it and give it to as many people that have a desire to see what you saw in Isaiah 6:1. I will lead you as I have led you to others." My attention turned to my present local church body, and I began thinking how to present this information to them. I heard the Lord speak; "Don't concern yourself with your thoughts. Give no attention to anything but learning to do what you see Father doing."

I was taken deeper still, where I saw things filthy, unimaginable deep dark secrets from Hell. I was told, "I have shown you this because you are called not to be unaware of the Devil's schemes. Most are not called to see this. Seal this information and let those I have called open this can of worms." When he said this, I saw a vision of many that were exposing evil. While looking into this realm, I was pulled out and told, "Stay focused on your task."

I was shown ways to restore the physical body, as well as the mind. I thought, "Some of this information I already know." The Lord responded to my thought, "I have ordered your steps son. All who call on the name of the Lord will be saved." The remainder of the information was mind-blowing. The totality of what needed to be done in the temple restoration process was too big to comprehend. Just as I became overwhelmed, a voice spoke. "I am here to help." I knew the voice had with him many others ready and willing to assist. He continued, "We are here to gather to you those who will eat the manna from Heaven. They will be clean enough vessels, able to anoint with authority, qualified to teach in the Kingdom, and implement the Will of the King in Heaven on earth."

In front of me was a great number of people who were teaching restoration material. I saw many books already written that were tools for rebuilding the temple. I knew some of the books were published and others were from the future. I thought to myself, "I hope my books will help." A voice spoke, "I will use your material, for you did not receive this from your own toil. Flesh and blood have not revealed this to you, but I have." Immediately a desire overtook me, and I wanted to "only do what I see my Father doing."

I found myself back at the throne. I felt the Lord taking pieces of my carnal mind and flesh from my heart. I saw him sowing it on the train of His robe. I knew there was much work to be done, but I was encouraged. I knew my time here was over. I bowed low before His throne. As I did, I was taken to a castle I knew to be somewhere in Europe. As I stood in front of it, I felt the acceptance of my Father as He showed me what He has been building in me.

CHAPTER THREE

HEAVEN ON EARTH

Experiences in the Non-Dual Nature of the Physical Realm and the Realm of the Kingdom

I saw a modern-day John the Baptist on the scene setting in motion a change of mind resulting in the formation of the renewed mind. The results of this transformation were unlike anything the earth had seen since the time of Christ and the Church's birth. His teaching I could see was a gift from Heaven. This "John the Baptist" appeared to be on the scene at the turn of the century and was pouring out from Heaven tools equipping the Saints to engage and ultimately discover their identity in the realm of Heaven. I saw a multitude of Saint's that possessed a piece of his mantle. Written on the mantles was, "understanding the Kingdom by seeking first the Kingdom." His teachings contained substance that carried away those assimilating and integrating the information of the Kingdom. They were being transported from a place on earth to a place in Heaven where they began learning to abide in their newly realized field of consciousness.

Saints were walking on earth, but I could clearly see they were in Heaven. I watched as suddenly they were transported to a specific place in Heaven, received information, and came back. I knew some were gone a moment, some were gone an hour; some were gone a day and some were gone a week. They were all living on earth in Heaven to varying degrees. It was like they were in two places simultaneously. It was then I understood superposition, entanglement, and other quantum mechanical principles on a new level.

I was granted access into realms of the Kingdom with a measure of free Will that scared me sober. I knew when I entered a new realm whether I was in the Lords Will or not. Other times, I was seized by an angel and taken places, given an assignment or shown something which I brought back and attempted to scribe. Most often, I was able to scribe each experience in real time. I knew this place to be the Kingdom of Heaven on earth and I knew I had found a dwelling place, not only for myself but for the Church Jesus is building.

"As long as I remain subject to the King, I will spend the rest of my life here," I thought. I also knew I could fall from here like lightning. I knew I wouldn't lose my salvation, just my privilege of helping usher in the Kingdom realm on earth. It's necessary to understand Jesus paid the price for our sins in full and has given us His righteousness, making us accepted forever. It is additionally important to understand that in the Kingdom on earth there is a practical cleansing and sanctifying necessary for all who desire to become Kingdom-dwellers. Jesus makes it clear in Revelation 3 that it's the overcomers who will rule and reign with Him on planet earth.

I witnessed a great multitude swept away into the kingdom of darkness because lust for the attributes of the Kingdom of Heaven disqualified them from partaking in the establishing of the Kingdom on earth. As I realized that selfish ambition dealt a death blow to many, grief surfaced in my emotions. A fear then rose up in me regarding those in the Kingdom stealing Kingdom content for selfish gain.

The spirit of Revelation appeared and downloaded a vision of the Kingdom that settled once and for all the impenetrable fortress guarding this massive, set apart Kingdom. There is nothing, "no thing" capable of stopping what the Lord wants done. The King truly holds all power, authority, and dominion. Anyone attempting such a foolish ploy would find themselves disqualified if confession, repentance, and change didn't happen. It was almost inconceivable that anyone would try such a thing, I thought. Then I remembered Satan falling from Heaven and was humbled. I realized just how inadequate the Church's attempts to establish the Kingdom were. I thought, "As long as the Church is functioning in the realm of the carnal mind She is powerless to co-labor with Christ to see His Kingdom come." It was then I realized that the Church Jesus is building is discovered in the field of Kingdom consciousness which requires the renewing of the mind in order to enter and their obedience to seeking first the Kingdom.

I saw two groups of "Kingdom" people. One group was living in Heaven on earth focused on the inner Kingdom, waiting for instructions from the King to begin moving the inner Kingdom structure and substance onto earth. When they did, it was swift, and His Kingdom swept across the earth quickly. I knew this to be years down the road (at least beyond 2025, possibly 2031 or later. That's not to say we won't see pop-up expressions of His Kingdom before then. How big those pop-up expressions will be is largely determined by the Saints.) This group had laser focus of seeking the Kingdom for the sole purpose of establishing its reign within them. They were paying no attention to expressing the Kingdom on earth but were resting in the Lords timing. Their character had matured to the degree they were willingly dying daily. I could see that this discipline had become a light burden. I could see some were embracing their cross affectionately as if they had an understanding of its necessity and were desperate not to let go. It was as if the cross had become a friend and loyal companion.

The other group I saw outside Heaven on earth. They were being used by God but were disqualified from the higher life of Heaven on earth due to selfish ambition, greed, lust for power, and other carnal characteristics not given over to the work of the crucifixion. Somewhere in the past they had left their cross and picked up fleshly desires that took over their identity. The irony was those carrying their cross in Heaven on earth were living a life in paradise-like fashion, while the others were in pain, strife, and suffering. The group living in paradise-like fashion had an understanding that "though our outward man perish, yet the inward man is renewed day by day" (2 Corinthians 4:16 KJV). They were focusing on the renewal taking place, knowing the perishing of the outward man was making the renewal possible. One group looked like Kingdom caterpillars and the other Kingdom Butterflies. The Kingdom caterpillars were demonstrating signs and wonders flowing from witchcraft, sorcery and demonic origins. I was told not to judge but rather discern and pray "thy Kingdom come."

As the kingdom of darkness was collapsing from within the human body, especially in the minds of humanity, I saw the inner Kingdom of Heaven arising. I knew I was witnessing the restoration of the temple. This restoration was making way for the influence and splendor of God to be seen on earth. I believe in the coming months and years great multitudes will be experiencing this inner Kingdom life, making way for great change upon the earth as well as in the hearts and minds of its inhabitants.

I was given a general time frame of events and was rebuked each time I tried to understand specific dates. There is information accessible in the Kingdom that is off limits. It is essential we surrender our free Will completely and continually over to Christ, co-laboring with Him to sanctify our entire being. Learning our role requires a renewing of the mind and a willingness only to do what we see the Lord doing.

From 2013-2031, God has specific activity planned. The Saints, once they receive Kingdom "sons of God" status, which is identity in Heaven, will need to be fully given over to the rule of Christ within. I saw this particular group being prepared when I was in a realm called "only doing what I see the Father doing." This realm I also call the "third rung on a ladder." I don't know how I came up with that title other than it showed up in the original scribed manuscript. There were only a few people present in this realm, but I knew multitudes would end up there. I knew those escorted into this realm where those seeking first the Kingdom. They had awareness of being in Heaven on earth. They understood and had been transformed in the mind to the degree they had conscious experience of the Kingdom on earth and had insight into righteousness. All persons in this realm had downloads of the aforementioned information, not merely a rudimentary understanding. The Spirit of Wisdom and Revelation had ruling authority over each Saint in this company. They didn't receive wisdom or revelation. They carried the Spirit of Wisdom and Revelation and made themselves available to them in the inner Kingdom. More than that, these Saints were conditioned to receive from them as a student attends to their teacher.

I understood the capstone of all such activity within the Kingdom manifesting on earth was minds being transformed as people passionately pursued understanding of the Kingdom of God and His righteousness. A change of mind resulting from seeking information of the Kingdom was the catalyst bringing transformation into their nature as "sons of God." Unity was also a major spark that ignited the fires of transformation.

There was such trust in the hearts of God's people. I found it hard to believe considering the depth of darkness around them. It was then that I received a revelation of the Kingdom that brought understanding of what I was seeing. Those that walk in the end time purposes of God will be settled in all things and live out of a deep state of rest. They will be firmly anchored in experiential understanding of the Kingdom's supreme authority over all the earth and its inhabitants, including themselves.

Jesus, King of all kings, is ruler overall and there is none like Him in Heaven or earth. No height or depth, nothing seen or unseen, can rival King Jesus. I saw that all power and authority combined was given by Him and was but a fraction of the totality of what He possessed. I saw the Mighty Ones who do His bidding effortlessly in complete rest, joyfully expanding awareness of the Kingdom like yeast making its way through dough.

"The Lord has established His throne in Heaven, and His Kingdom rules over all. Praise the Lord, you his angels, you mighty ones who do his bidding, who obey his word. Praise the Lord, all his heavenly hosts you his servants who do his will. Praise the Lord, all his works everywhere in his dominion"
Psalm 103.19-22

I saw written on the soles of the feet of every Saint in Heaven "seeking first the Kingdom is the key."

I observed the earth beginning to fill with the influence of God. There were keys that unlocked ways to begin "filling up the earth with His influence." They were placed in me, and I was told to seal them up for a later time. I saw the keys of the Kingdom were given to those seeking first the Kingdom, but it was Christ in them who had the authority to use them. It was as if the disciples were given the keys for the purpose of giving them back to Jesus. I saw the coming together of the Church and the ways in which the King chose to prepare His temple, His Body on earth. I saw the corporate temple, individuals gathering together and building up one another, while preparing the corporate body. Great emphasis was placed on establishing the Kingdom within the individual.

I saw the kingdom of darkness collapsing as the restored temple discovered its identity through the placing on of eye salve and the removal of cataracts. This triggered both sight and vision of the Kingdom and in the Kingdom, first, within the individual temple, then outwardly through the cooperate temple of the Church. Then the whole earth was becoming His temple. There was great caution given to the Saints not to begin establishing the Kingdom on earth yet, but to remain inward, allowing the King to establish rule in the individual temple first.

Heaven contains countless volumes of information. In certain realms I visited, when I saw something, the information contained in what was seen, instantly revealed itself to me. Hence, awareness of something took that which was in my vision and deposited it in me, spilling out the information it contained and bringing instant awareness and revelatory insight.

I knew the emphasis for the present was on leaders seeking first the Kingdom. The revelation I received (which was described in my chapter on disciples in my book *Discovering the Kingdom*) was key to causing an earthly wild fire of seeking first the Kingdom Saints. I felt all revivals on earth initially were for the purpose of bringing the message of the Kingdom—the message of seeking first the Kingdom. I thought the less emotional the leadership, the more likely the move might be from Heaven. The more focus on bringing understanding of the Kingdom and emphasis on seeking first the Kingdom, the more likely it was Heavens doing. I saw many "revivals" that were birthed out of soulish, selfish ambition, and even out of hell.

I prayed for Saints to be plucked out from under that spell of false-revivalists. I pray mercy on the leaders to get their focus back on Heaven's work. Out of those participating in Heaven's revival, multitudes would be caught, captured, and consumed by the Kingdom. These would become the leaders in the coming Kingdom Church. Those crowned disciples are entrusted with discipling nations. Those caught, captured, and consumed Kingdom Saints are alive on earth today and will need to gather together under specific direction from the King before the Kingdom comes in a fashion that begins changing Nations.

I saw many gathering places in Heaven on earth. I also saw "roundtable" gatherings where the glory of the Lord shined on the faces of those in attendance like Moses after leaving God's presence. What I saw became part of me. The mind of Christ formed in the Saints produced an instant download of the information being received. The principle of the progression of "knowledge—understanding—wisdom" had been overtaken by a higher law, a law of the Spirit of the life of Christ in the crucified life of the Saint. I saw the Spirit of Wisdom and Revelation coming and going in the Church age, and I saw the Spirit of Wisdom and Revelation resting in the Saints living in the Kingdom age. This has begun.

I saw a ladder whose first rung was off the earth in Heaven. I knew it was a "Heaven on earth ladder." I saw many rungs from bottom to top. The first rung was "Seek first the Kingdom." The second rung was "Seek first His righteousness," and the third, "Seek only to do what you see the Father doing." The fourth rung was blank.

I became discouraged. Then the Spirit of Wisdom motioned to me, and I followed. I was shown much destruction and was told, "If you move past these three rungs you will cause that destruction. I was then taken to a high place where I saw more destruction. The Spirit spoke, "This destruction is too late for you to do anything about." I knew what caused it and became upset. "Be of good cheer! replied the Spirit. You know all shaking is a shaking towards the everlasting Kingdom." My desire was still strong to avoid as much trouble on earth as possible when I heard the Lord respond, "I will remember this, My son." Joy filled me as I took a deep breath.

I saw the distinction between the natural and spiritual realm blurring in the restored temple until the two became one. I heard a voice say, "Welcome to the Kingdom within! You can stay here all you want as long as righteousness prevails." I knew what he meant and thought, "Is anyone else here yet? I sure am lonely and would like to meet other Saints up here." Wisdom moved towards me and replied, "More than you think. Holy Spirit will bring them to you in His timing." Suddenly, before me was the most influential smile I've ever seen. I knew it was Holy Spirit. We connected on a level of intimacy I never knew existed.

I saw Royal Kingdom Family walking on the earth as "Jacob's ladder" was put in them. They were not ascending and descending Heaven to earth as they were no longer in the earth. They were in Heaven on earth. They were being moved from one place in the heavenlies to another place, Heaven on earth. There was no evil here, as all darkness was closed off. As long as I remained "quick to repent" I was safe. "If you drink any deadly poison in this realm it will not harm you," came a voice I knew to be Holy Spirit. I replied, "I like you! No, I love you Holy Spirit!"

He replied, "I look forward to walking with you. We have much work to do. Keep your task in mind."

I saw Saints who found an environment where authenticity was encouraged. From that environment, an explosion of Kingdom awareness, activity, and demonstration took place. I knew those Saints to be "seeded" with the "seeking first the Kingdom seed" and life was springing forth from the seed. I recalled Jehu's need for a friend's encouragement. In 2 Kings 9, Elisha summoned a prophet from his school and sent him to find a man named Jehu. The prophet was asked to separate Jehu from his friends, anoint him with oil and prophesy "I anoint you King over Israel." After receiving the word, Jehu returned to his friends. They asked him what the prophet said. Jehu's insecurities and disbelief toward the greatness of his calling caused him to respond in a manner that dismissed the prophecy. But his friends insisted on hearing what was told him, so Jehu answered, "Here is what he told me: "This is what the Lord says: I anoint you king over Israel." Upon hearing this, Jehu's friends began treating him like a king and proclaiming "Jehu is king!" In order for Jehu to step into his calling, the Lord needed to send friends to awaken and "call forth" the destiny lying dormant within him!

Kingdom Saints will begin stepping into relationships where friends call forth destiny to the point where it's almost a commission release. This anointing I knew had been released to leaders for the building up of the body. "Be discerning when releasing this anointing," said Holy Spirit. When He spoke, I felt tingling in my hands and knew I was going to see many touched by this infusion of vision and awareness coming from the simplicity of Kingdom encouragement.

Author's Note: I want to emphasize, this relationship did not generate commission release. It was just very impactful and appeared to. Scripture lays out clear protocol for releasing Saints to function in their gifting. I've found several of these protocols in the book of Acts. Additionally, the Lord is the ultimate authority on who and when a person is released. He will confirm His decision and timing with His leadership. Heaven has a culture of honor, respect, and a clear directional path affirmed by two or more in leadership.

Multitudes stood outside the Kingdom wanting a taste of what was happening but were unable. Their foreheads were not marked "seeking first the Kingdom." When my eyes connected with another man's, wisdom regarding strategy for bringing in those outside the Kingdom was transferred to me. I thought "I never had that type of download. Why did this take place when my eyes made contact with another?" Holy Spirit responded, "Because your eyes are the window to your soul. A key to bringing in those outside of the Kingdom is a permeation of love resting in your entire soul." I asked, "How does this happen?" He responded, "Into me you see." I knew He meant intimacy. I knew the more time spent in the bed chambers of the King, the greater infusion of love. My affections were swept away, and I found myself locked "into me you see" with Him.

I observed individual leaders receiving a revelation. It contained books of information in that one revelation. They handed the revelation to others in the Kingdom who received the book to write. It was Divine Kingdom transference. I watched books being downloaded in Kingdom Saints instantly. The Lord gave someone a revelation, and when he received it, the contents in the revelation opened to him. He said, "Write, for now is the time of information infusion." There was more information in that one revelation than I could imagine—hundreds of thousands if not millions of books in one revelation.

I witnessed two Kingdom Saints came together. One was taken into another realm where a piece of information became a book. Each piece of information received, turned into a book and was downloaded in the "self." There were scribes anointed to write what was downloaded in the messenger. The scribe received the information through divine transference within the piece of information. I thought to myself, "How can the Kingdom contain this amount of information? We will be writing new information for eternity!" Wisdom interrupted, "Keep the task in mind young man. You need to teach the scribes how to learn to differentiate the most important information downloaded in order to maximize Heaven's effect on earth." I thought to myself, "How on earth am I going to find these scribes?" The moment I thought this, I realized I did not have the mind of Christ in that thought. It was carnal and outside my sphere of influence. I confessed, and Wisdom continued, "In the future, I will give you awareness of who to lay your hands on for this wisdom to be transferred. Until then, feel safe and secure."

I was taken to a bridge where I saw the evil of industry as it colluded to destroy the temple with toxins. I saw the veil lifted from the mystery of "I will make those who are of the synagogue of Satan, who claim to be Jews though they are not, but are liars—I will make them come and fall down at your feet and acknowledge that I have loved you" (Revelation 3:9, NIV). I heard the Lord say, "Seal up this scroll for the time being. All manner of evil is to be ignored in this season. My Saints are wasting valuable time. I want all devotion possible spent on seeking first the Kingdom within."

When He said this, I saw Heaven's ladder and the entire Church standing on one of the three rungs. Many outside the Church were off the ladder wanting on. Some were beyond the third rung outside the Lords Will. I heard, "They are in danger. Beckon them to come down." Immediately I prayed and some came down, but some didn't. "Seal up what you just saw and remember this next time you're tempted to move beyond my Will." I became very sober and searched for Holy Spirit. He appeared before me with a bigger smile than ever. As I began to cry, He spoke, "Be of good cheer! The King has sent Me to make you an overcomer. I will be your helper." As He said this, I saw a measure of the bigness of the Kingdom that caused me to wish I could enter the eternal Kingdom now.

I was taken to a room that felt ancient. I knew it to be full of life and wisdom. It was a different wisdom than the Spirit of Wisdom carried. Suddenly, Paul the Apostle appeared and said "Michael! It is far better to be absent from the body, but you have such opportunity while on earth. All of creation has been waiting since the fall in the Garden for what you are helping to usher in. Hold fast, my brother! Keep the faith! Run the race!" We hugged, and when we did, I felt energy touch my body. I was escorted off, but not before drinking what appeared to be water from the river of life. I wanted to inquire but knew it was not for me to know. I then found myself in the bed chambers of the Lord aroused with love towards Him. I knew it was from the water of life I'd just drunk. I also knew it was a test to see if I would pierce into the future beyond His Will. "Well done," replied a cheery fellow I'd never met. I knew he was from the future. He kept his identity hidden but promised, "You will see me later." I smiled, and he left.

I was taken to a period of time I felt was in the near future. It seemed to be in 2018 or 2019. I saw a man standing outside a hospital emergency room. As people were coming in, he stretched forth his hand, and they were healed. I heard the cries of what I felt were coming from Zion, Illinois. I knew the voice to be John Alexander Dowie. I thought, "Is this the man that was imprisoned many times for his faith? With a happy smile, he appeared and replied "Why yes, that is true. And look at me now!!" I laughed in amazement and thought, "This place is absolutely amazing! I can't even begin to comprehend …" Suddenly I was interrupted by, "Keep the task in mind. You will have eternity to excite your emotions." I agreed, and John left.

I then saw seeds from Zion being hurled over the earth and was told, "Seal this up for now. You will be asked to release this in the future. There is enough premature 'Kingdom' activity already." I became sober and replied, "Yes sir." I thought, "I never met him before. I presume he is from the future. He was a sober fellow, one who knows how to be about the Father's business."

I was taken a little further down the road of time where I saw a man that was writing down information. It became obsolete by the time he finished because time in the Kingdom on earth was speeding up so fast. It's not that the information was wrong or bad, in fact, it was insightful Kingdom revelation. The awareness of the Kingdom in the Church was accelerating so fast that by the time it had written down a Kingdom law it was superseded by another remarkable revelation of the Kingdom.

I heard a voice, "You have already experienced this dimension with your spiritual father to a degree. I will begin releasing this on a grander scale. Once more Saints are being swept into and being established in the Kingdom. Keep blowing the trumpet of seeking the Kingdom first."

I wanted to ask several questions but felt it was not appropriate. "Trust those who have experienced this and fear not. Watch and pray!" More information for the future was given to me, and I heard the Father say, "You are a beloved son in whom I am well pleased." As He said this, Jesus appeared beside me. He was much larger than me and very joyous. He put His arm around me and said nothing. I could feel His love and acceptance. It fueled me to love and accept others and inspired me to keep going.

I saw the parable of the workers (Matthew 20:1-16) being played out as it related to dispensing information of the Kingdom onto earth. I saw those that worked on "seeking first the Kingdom" for years dispensing their acquired wisdom into new Kingdom Saints willing to receive the "seeking first the Kingdom mantle" and the new Saints being equal in faith level to those "working" for years. A voice spoke, "Make sure your hearts are prepared for this."

Author's Note: Matthew 20 is the story of a land owner who hires workers to work his vineyard. He hires workers at different times of the day. At the end of the day, he pays all the workers the same wage no matter the time spent laboring. In Heaven, faith is its currency, therefore no matter how much time you've been laboring in the Kingdom, faith is being distributed by the King equally. Those working longer need to accept this to maintain unity in the body of Christ.

I saw humans with bullet proof vests embedded in their skin used in man's earthly conflict of greed, power, fame, and lust. I heard the Lord speak, "Don't get entangled in earthly government affairs. Get and stay connected with My Government. Keep seeking first the Kingdom." I turned and saw Kingdom Saints with the same "bullet proof vest" in their skin only it was used as supernatural protection against all the fiery darts of the evil one. It was made from peace and rest and produced more peace and rest the longer it was worn. I asked the Lord, "Who gets these vests?" He told me, "They are given to those who possess Kingdom faith." It was then I realized this was the shield of faith for the Kingdom Saints.

> *"In addition, take up the shield of faith, with which you can*
> *extinguish all the flaming arrows of the evil one."*
> Ephesians 6:16, BSB

This, along with "the bubble" which is what I saw many Mighty One's walking in, were Kingdom garments reserved for the Saints in the midst of collapsing the kingdom of darkness and bringing collective consciousness of the Kingdom of light. I was warned, "Keep your focus off works of darkness and the outward Kingdom and on the task at hand."

I saw the pioneer Kingdom Saints carrying information relating to the Internet, WiFi, cell phones, and other devices of like kind. They were using the information as teaching tools that helped bring Kingdom understanding to future Saints by awakening conscious experience of the Kingdom in them. This information was also used to bring greater desire and pursuit of the Kingdom to the Saints. Information regarding the outworkings of wave frequencies in the air is key bits of knowledge that will help paint a picture of the means in which the invisible Kingdom has lasting effect on earth.

I saw the lives of many Saints shortened by ignorance as disease took over their bodies. The Lord took me back in time and showed me companies and entire industries where Satan erected his business of stealing, killing, and destroying in attempts to slow down the rise of God's Kingdom in man. I heard the Lord say "I save My best work for last and your lives are being cut short. The premature deterioration of your body has kept Me from performing My greatest works. Your body which is really My body is defiled (1 Corinthians 6:12-20). Cleanse, rebuild, and restore, and I will dwell in your midst and through your midst in Kingdom fashion. You've picked up My mind, and now I need a place to lay My head" (read Matthew 8:20). I knew "picked up My mind" to mean Jesus' top priority for mankind: seeking first the Kingdom.

My grief turned to astonishment as I saw this premature death cycle broken, the temple restored, and the sons of God walking the earth in Heaven. The purity expressing itself from these restored bodies was divine, full of life and light. I heard a company of Saints expressing concern as to how they would make themselves that pure. I opened my mouth and before I could speak the Lord answered, "All Saints in the Kingdom who desire purity will be healed like no earthly mind has conceived." The Saints heard this and responded, "How do we see the Kingdom?" I said, "Make it our number one priority to seek the Kingdom." Suddenly stacks of books appeared. I recognized many of them. Before I could respond, I vanished. While being transported out of this place, the Holy Spirit said, "Remember you're in the realm of 'only doing what you see the Father doing.' Stay connected with your task." I agreed and found myself before an old worn down building.

As I approached the building, it multiplied and was converted into churches. I could see inside despite being outside. The Church was defiled, but the presence of the Lord was heavy in Her midst. I asked the Lord about this, and He said, "The flesh can carry My presence: look at the Philistines. My Saints must pick up their cross and carry it daily." Suddenly a voice from the earth cried out. "Never forget this moment. You are standing on the earth. I have taken you out from Heaven momentarily." I scratched my head and began thinking out of my carnal mind. I felt evil and saw caterpillars trying to crawl up my legs. I took a deep breath, held it and wished I was back in Heaven. The voice from the earth responded, "Let this be an incentive to pursue only doing what you see the Father doing. The more accurate you become in expressing what the Father's doing, the more effect you will have for the Kingdom." I was energized, and just prior to returning to the throne I saw a sign that said, "Pray for teachers who will seek first the Kingdom." I knew that was the present predominant cry of Heaven for earth.

I saw the Kingdom of Heaven being established first within individuals through a transformation by the renewal of the mind and body, then, in the earth through the Lords influence by way of the Church. Everything was being gathered into one of two groups: the Kingdom of darkness and the Kingdom of light. The Kingdom of light was triumphing in the midst of gross darkness.

Author's Note: Too often there is a mad rush to see the outward manifestation of the Kingdom void of inward awareness and establishment. I'm concerned this will produce a superficiality that may cause this group to be swept into a false kingdom of hype, witchcraft, and sorcery flowing from the soulish works of the flesh. Let this serve as a warning to examine where you are looking for the Kingdom. Those who do not first discover the Kingdom within are prone to seek the benefits of the Kingdom and the things of the Kingdom that fulfill their own appetites (see John 6:26).

We are living in an age of unprecedented enlightenment, especially as it relates to the exposure of the works of darkness and its antidote, the Kingdom of light. It only takes a small band of unified Kingdom Saints for the Lord to collapse governments of nations. This is both encouraging and empowering as it enlarges our belt of truth and enables us to step into Kingdom dimensions. Right information—the information received while seeking first the Kingdom—is a stepping stone to Kingdom expression. No longer do the self-appointed guardians of the key of knowledge hold authority. The stronghold of ignorance is being broken and has begun sweeping the globe like a holy virus. The more we take hold of the key of knowledge which is the information of the Kingdom, the freer we become from the prison of ignorance. The freer we become from the prison of ignorance the more the Kingdom field of consciousness appears in our subjective experience. The influence of darkness is being neutralized as the information of the Kingdom is once again being sought after. The means by which the kingdom of darkness has kept people from entering the Kingdom of light is shattering. It's time for the Saints to arise and shine. It's high time the glorious influence of the Lord be put back in His temple—the sons and daughters of God.

Because the human body was chosen by God to be His dwelling place on earth, it preoccupies the kingdom of darkness preeminently. We must stop giving attention to outward things and give ourselves over to understanding His temple, our bodies. Satan has no greater devotion than to defile our body, mind, and spirit. He does this primarily by blinding the mind (1 Corinthians 4:4) and poisoning the body. The result is death by ignorance and a life that culminates in premature physical death. In doing so, he inhibits the manifestation of God's governing rulership on earth. While the unleashing of the destruction of the body has intensified, the antidote is being emphasized like never before. The thief has been caught. The original temple blueprint has been found, and the robbers are being exposed, setting the stage for the return of the glory and splendor of God. Once the Church understands Her purpose as the temple of God, and recognizes Her present defiled condition, the restoration will speed up.

We are living in the days of temple restoration. Preparing a dwelling place for the Lord is the King's priority. In this season, wise men and women are choosing to prepare themselves to be vessels fit for the King's use. They will be given a rudimentary understanding of the defilement that has taken place in their bodies. They will understand and recognize the robbers that have stolen from and altered the original blueprints and become willing to co-labor with the Lord to restore His temple. These men and women will be equipped with the proper tools and right building materials to make room for the splendor and majesty of God flowing through them. Additionally, an authority on earth will emerge that will draw families, cities, and governments to the Kingdom Church. A genuine longing to know the secrets of the Church's power and authority will surface in many, while a vengeful disdain will further enrage those representing the systems of this world. The stage is being set for the ultimate clash between two kingdoms. Tryouts and auditions have begun as the eyes of the Lord are running to and fro throughout the whole earth. Consider your role. Prepare for your scene. The time is now.

The weight of the power and presence of God flowing out of a group of restored people will provide supernatural provision for entire cities as the culture of Heaven awakens in the consciousness of the inhabitants of the earth. The attributes of the government of Heaven seen throughout scripture are coming alive in our generation. In the midst of great chaos will arise places of oasis. It's important to keep in mind, "all shaking is a shaking towards the Kingdom of God." These supernatural oases will provide safety and provision for those seeking first the Kingdom of God. But not before we "get wisdom and get understanding."

"Wisdom is supreme: therefore get wisdom. Yes, though it cost all your possessions, get understanding."
Proverbs 4:7 WEB
There is much transformation ahead. This transformation

requires a willing heart, moldable mind, and a resounding yes in one's spirit.

"The Spirit and the bride say, "Come!" Let the one who hears say, "Come!" And let the one who is thirsty come, and the one who desires the water of life drink freely."

Revelation 22:17, BSB

The work assigned to the Lord's laborers will be a satisfying and fulfilling labor of love.

The two years I spent having daily encounters in the third heaven were special. When the Lord took that privilege away, I thought I just lost the greatest gift outside salvation. I was wrong. God gave me those two years of "having experiences" and those experiences transformed my life to a degree. Now I'm "living an experience" almost continually. I've entered a Kingdom state of mind which contains conscious experience of the Kingdom on earth as opposed to conscious experience of the systems of this world. To a large degree, I've left the realm of the carnal world and have entered the realm of Kingdom consciousness.

We all want supernatural experiences. We were created from the spiritual realm. We came, not from our mother's womb but the Fathers' heart. In fact, we are a spirit in a body. That's our true nature. In the Kingdom, God doesn't want us to have occasional supernatural experiences; He wants our lives to become one big supernatural experience—a union between the physical realm and the realm of the Kingdom, a life lived as one big indescribably, peaceful, supernatural experience.

Jesus came and provided abundant life not made up of things but states of being. Those who seek first the Kingdom will be those who are transported into the conscious experience of the abundant life realized in the Kingdom realm of consciousness. "What no eye has seen, what no ear has heard and what no human mind has conceived the things God has prepared for those who love Him—these are the things God has revealed to us by his Spirit ... For, who has known the mind of the Lord so as to instruct him? But we have the mind of Christ." (Read 1 Corinthians 2: 9-16).

Overcoming the Ignorance of the Age

I was a drug attic who sobered up in 1991. I took drugs because of the feelings it produced as well as its mind altering and mood-altering effects. I can tell you that living in the conscious experience of Heaven on earth is so much better. Don't pursue an experience, pursue the Kingdom and you will end up living the rest of your life in one continuous experience. Seek first the Kingdom until you're given a revelation. My friend said it well, "Once you have discovered the Kingdom and seen it, then you will continue to seek it." This is where Jesus is taking His Church!

Understanding is an essential foundation to everything in life. "My people perish for lack of knowledge" is a principle laid before mankind (Hosea 4:7). Right knowledge leads to life while ignorance results in death. Right knowledge produces freedom while ignorance brings enslavement. The richest storehouse of right knowledge is discovered once a decision is made to seek first the Kingdom of God and His righteousness. As the Church, we have been an ignorant people. Ignorant of the information responsible for opening the realm of Kingdom consciousness to our subjective experience. This ignorance has resulted in enslavement to Satan's kingdom. Presently, the Church is under the principles and laws that govern the kingdom of darkness.

Instead of coming out of these systems we have migrated into them. Choosing to eat from the "good" part of the Tree of the Knowledge of Good and Evil, we have forfeited the life God designed for us. Instead of coming under the authority of the government of Heaven we have become enslaved to the principles of this world. Satan's kingdom has permeated our bodies and minds, resulting in a life lived out of his kingdom.

His culture, social norms, and mindsets have fashioned our minds away from awareness of God's Kingdom, blinding us from it.

Since the body is a vessel, containing both kingdoms, we choose, through the information we receive, which kingdom collapses and which one is erected. If the Kingdom of God is within but not visible to both the eyes of our understanding and our physical eyes, then Satan's kingdom is the kingdom standing. You don't have to see demons, fallen angels, and works of darkness to see Satan's kingdom. Remember, he comes as an angel of light—a wolf in sheep's clothing.

Presently, the Church is largely governed by Satan's world system of rulership. This should come as no surprise since the earthly Church has always been recognized as one of many world religions. Consequently, the thief has come and stolen from us God's intention for us, which is to live under His Kingdom and His rulership.

We have not chosen to eat from the Tree of Life. There fore, Satan has succeeded in tearing down our bodies rendering the temple of God ineffective. God designed our bodies to house His presence. They are meant to be a "building" where He can display His splendor and majesty on earth. A conduit through which He may represent His nature, culture, and social norms on earth just like it is in Heaven.

Today, our bodies are largely toxic waste dumps carrying disease and defilement. Closed off from the awareness of the Kingdom, we have crawled on the earth like a caterpillar as we've lived our existence from the realm of the carnal mind. Through our ignorance, Satan has turned God's vision upside down. Our brains have been wiped clean of the physical substrates responsible for consciousness in the Kingdom. This has resulted in the dismantling of the renewed mind and in its place the information of good and evil has awakened us to a world outside the King's domain. Now is the time to repent, for the Kingdom of Heaven is at hand. Arise! Shine, for the influence of the Lord is rising. The longer we remain seeking first the Kingdom, the more aware we become of the Kingdom and its influence—first in our personal lives, then on earth.

We must come to grips with our ignorance. We must learn from king Ahaz, who surrendered himself to the influence of idolatry. Because of this, the light that once shined bright in the Temple was shut off (2 Chronicles 29:7). In these days, we've given ourselves over to the influences of chemicals never designed for our bodies and belief systems never created for our minds. We have substituted the discipline of seeking the Kingdom for a myriad of other acts. Just as God raised up Hezekiah to restore the temple, so too has he raised up a restoring people today. I saw the restored temple, and its magnificence is beyond comprehension. I knew it was in the future, but I also knew the keys to restoration were back in the hands of a group of disciples that will not disappoint Heaven or earth.

If Jesus commanded us to seek first the Kingdom, then we must come to grips with the fact that if we are not, then we are practicing idolatry. This narrow mindset is difficult to consider. Nonetheless, if king Ahaz lost his light due to idolatry, then we must consider it possible that we can lose our light—Kingdom consciousness—when we cease to seek first the Kingdom. This single fact, once reckoned, will prove to be the switch that turns on the temple light! All building materials for the restoration of the temple are found and accessed while seeking first the Kingdom. In fact, the very discipline of seeking first the Kingdom is the act of restoring the temple. Revelation of the Kingdom builds the house ("upon this rock, I will build my Church …").

Our bodies are the Lord's temple. Yet, its present condition is a dwelling place of robbers. Restoring the body is the means to rebuilding the temple of God. This change is a requirement for the Overcomers. A set of standards is laid out to begin this process. Identifying specific thieves and replacing necessary items is the task. This will make way for the coming of the Lord through the Mighty Ones. Those with a cleansed temple are positioned to stand and minister in the day of the Lord. The weight and power the Lord is bringing to earth demands we rebuild the temple His way. Without restoration, we will misrepresent Him. Without the discipline of seeking first the Kingdom, the Lord cannot provide us with the ingredients required to awaken us to the beauty of His Kingdom experientially.

ONE FINAL PERSONAL EXPERIENCE

As I was reading a friend's email, I went into a transformational experience. The Lord transported me into a realm where volumes of books sat, waiting to be written. It appears three or four might have fallen into me. I believe it to be a realm of the "Oracles of God" or a Heavenly library with hundreds if not thousands of books waiting to be written. It felt like I was in the mind of Christ and this library was a compartment of His mind. In this realm, I perceived revelation untold, mysteries beyond thought, beyond comprehension, waiting to be picked up and brought into existence. I'm not sure if I've entered this realm, if it's been downloaded into me, or perhaps I'm just visiting. It seems, as one enters certain realms in Heaven, one becomes what's contained in that realm as awareness is awakened and enlarged. It's beautiful beyond description. It's clear to me the glory and splendor of the Lord will be revealed in and through His temple. Both the individual and corporate Body of Christ is indescribably filled with unstoppable influence and authority. This Kingdom is BIG! Much bigger than I'd ever imagined and the King has EVERYTHING under His control! WOW, this is breathtaking, astonishingly beautiful!

My friend made the comment, "It absolutely exploded my mind." He was referencing an experience he had while reading my email. As I read his statement, something happened to the back of my brain, perhaps in the parietal lobe. It wasn't like anything I had ever felt before, and there's nothing I could identify it with. Even as I write, I have no language to explain it. The best I can do is say I felt a billion tingles within that specific part of my brain. There have been three benefits I've discovered from the experience: 1) My writing has gone to a new level; 2) my Kingdom experience within my Kingdom living has gone to new heights; 3) and my soul and body have experienced a cleansing. I attribute this experience to a synergy that will begin taking place more and more as Saints seeking first the Kingdom come together. I note this as a documentation, not as any prerequisite to moving forward with God. Jesus dealt with our sin, and we have been made the righteousness of God in Christ. We must not shrink back by trying to perfect in the flesh what has begun in the Spirit. Practical holiness is a work of the Spirit, never a striving of the flesh. Settle this in your mind and heart. Rehearse it in your mind until revelation of divine empowerment becomes the fortress of your conscious experience.

Author's Note: I believe we have stepped into uncharted waters, at least since the early Church fathers. Revelation that continues to be downloaded, as well as experiences in the Kingdom, are providing a template for the Church to "come up here," not as an experience but rather a way of life. The above mentioned experience with my friend serves as a down payment for those relationships centered on seeking first the Kingdom. Do not be surprised when revelatory encounters increase as we come together with others seeking first the Kingdom. Rather rejoice in the fact that the content within the unity of mind created by our assembly is beginning to express itself!

CHAPTER FOUR

Rewiring the Brain for Kingdom Compatibility

The Appearing of the Kingdom realm in Our Conscious Experience—The Key which Opens the Kingdom

I was taken to a place like no other. There was more awe and majesty than I've ever experienced. Written in the atmosphere was "in the beginning God." I knew this place to be the mind of Christ. My attention turned to what appeared to be another mind growing in the mind of Christ.

Suddenly, I was interrupted by the smell of joy, and a voice spoke out of the fragrance, "Your friend was right. You have been given seminal information from the Father. This is reserved for a few for the time being." I asked, "For who?" Immediately, I was taken back to the time I received the revelation on "disciples" in 2015. While traveling there, I could feel many names being downloaded in the back of my head.

Footnote: You can read about this revelation in my book, *Discovering the Kingdom*. I devoted a chapter to disciples, explaining what one is and their importance in the dawning of the Kingdom on earth.

I arrived back in time and there before me was a book. Written inside were the names of those to initially receive this information for the purpose of pioneering the pathway to conscious experience of the Kingdom on earth. I couldn't see the names, but I knew it was not for me to know. "You are correct," the voice responded to my thoughts. "Those walking under the conditions of a disciple will be given this manna. Those walking in the field of seeking first the Kingdom are in for a treat." I was remembering the acceleration in Kingdom awareness my spiritual father and I had been experiencing when the voice continued, "Keep writing. I want you to begin offering this to the lost sheep of the House of Israel. You know where they are." "Yes," I answered. As soon as I did, I saw an explosion and knew that was the effect this information was having in the Saints. It was an explosion of transformation through the renewing of the mind. A voice spoke to me, "Make sure unity goes with this." Suddenly, a revelation containing volumes of books was released. I thought, "The world is changing rapidly." When I saw this, I was brought back to the present and heard the Lord say, "Keep in mind the task at hand; seek first My Kingdom, seek first My righteousness, and seek to only do what you see Me doing."

I was taken back to the mind of Christ where my attention was directed to the other mind growing in Christ's mind. I knew this mind represented all the minds of the pioneer Saints, the first of the Kingdom-dwellers. I looked closer, and when I did, I became sick and threw up. "Why did this happen?" I thought. "How can something so corrupt live in a place so perfect?" I heard a voice, "We are here to change this. Watch." What I saw I have no words for. It was like trillions of actions and transactions taking place at once. I asked, "What is this?" The voice responded, "This is the brain." Suddenly, the connections and transactions began separating and divorcing. I saw a courtroom where the judge declared a verdict and rendered a divorce. I saw an execution room with what appeared to be the cloud of witnesses cheering as billions of actions and transactions were killed. I was witnessing the renewing of the mind, and I could see two activities taking place simultaneously. The neuron connections that birthed the carnal mind were being separated, and the separation was causing a death of the carnal mind. I also witnessed new neuron marriages which were giving birth to a new field of conscious experience as evidenced by the appearing of the renewed mind. The new mind was bringing awareness of the Kingdom through the appearing of the Kingdom field of consciousness. The mind that made me sick just a moment ago was being overshadowed by a new mind that was taking those with a renewed mind into another world, the world of the Kingdom on earth.

My attention turned back to the mind of Christ, and I saw the mind of the Saints continuing to grow. I asked the Lord, "What was that? What just took place?" He responded, "Repentance." I thought, "Impossible." Immediately, a voice spoke, "No mind has yet to conceive what God has in store for those who change their mind with seeking first the Kingdom material."

Then I was taken to a shipyard where I saw a fleet of ships sinking. The voice spoke, "When Saint's drown their fleshly attention and devote themselves to seeking first the Kingdom, they will begin to see this." Suddenly I was moved high above the earth. As the voice directed my attention down, he placed a chair before me and said, "Sit." I knew I was in for a treat. The voice interrupted my thought, "I gave you the chair because no man can see what I'm about to show you unless he is seated, for standing in this glory under any carnal strength is impossible." Suddenly, a bolt of lightning struck my chest, and I died but was alive.

When I looked down, I first noticed I was outside of time. The voice spoke, "What I'm about to show you can only materialize in the Kingdom Saints who live outside time." I took a deep breath, and the voice responded, "You're ready." I said, "OK." As He was about to bring awareness to me of something, I realized the voice was Holy Spirit. I saw His smile and immediately knew. He smiled and opened my awareness. I then found myself at the throne face down. All was still. Darkness and silence were around the throne. I had never seen this and thought to myself, "What is happening?"

Faintly, off in the distance, I heard what I knew was part of Isaiah 6:1-8 (NIV) being sung.

"... I saw the Lord, high and exalted, seated on a throne and the train of his robe filled the temple. Above him were seraphim, each with six wings. With two wings they covered their faces, with two, they covered their feet, and with two they were flying. And they were calling to one another: 'Holy, Holy, Holy is the Lord Almighty; the whole earth is full of his glory.' At the sound of their voices, the doorposts and thresholds shook, and the temple was filled with smoke. 'Woe to me!' I cried. 'I am ruined! For I am a man of unclean lips, and I live among a people of unclean lips, and my eyes have seen the King, the Lord Almighty.' Then one of the seraphim flew to me with a live coal in his hand, which he had taken with tongs from the altar. With it, he touched my mouth and said, 'See, this has touched your lips; your guilt is taken away, and your sin atoned for.' Then I heard the voice of the Lord saying, 'Whom shall I send? And who will go for us?' And I said, 'Here am I. Send me!'"

When the last frame was sung, "Here I am. Send me!"I was suddenly back before the mind of Christ.

This time I was at a different vantage point. When I looked inside, I saw the mind of the Saint grow and become a miniature replica of the mind of Christ. The only difference was written on his forehead: "Jesus Christ is Lord of lords and King of kings." I became so overwhelmed I had to rest. The voice took me to the throne, and I was given what looked like gold transmuted to its purest form. I heard the Lord say, "Trust not in this world." After He spoke, I felt a touch in my mind, and a voice said, "You have been given the key to entrance into the mind of Christ. Never fear, this place and all other places in the Kingdom are locked. Only those with keys can enter." I knew this key to entrance into the mind of Christ to be the transformation of our minds by seeking first of the Kingdom. I knew the key to entrance was to conform the mind to the patterns of the Kingdom by taking in the information of the Kingdom.

My attention was turned, and I saw a "John the Baptist" of my day. I motioned to him as if to say thank you, but he knew my thoughts before I could say anything. He smiled, nodded his head and thought back to me, "Good job." I wanted to ask him many questions when a voice spoke, "Not now. Stay focused on the task at hand." Suddenly, information became available to me that was comforting, very comforting. I was told to seal it for now and get back to the throne. Before leaving, I looked down and before me were three number eights. I knew them to represent the mind of Christ being formed in the Saints who were in the Kingdom, creating a new beginning for eternity.

As I returned to the throne, I thought of my spiritual father's concern about seminal information being disseminated correctly and timely. I knew this to be wise. A voice spoke reassuringly to me, "Only those in the Kingdom are given Kingdom keys." When he said this, I was taken back to the initial revelation I received of the bigness of the King and His all-powerfulness. I realized, "No one can manipulate the information of the Kingdom. The Kingdom is so protected! The path into the Kingdom is narrow, only those walking the path will enter." I saw in the distance a path and suspended above it was the word "start here." I knew that represented the renewing of the mind that would begin as we seek first of the Kingdom.

EXPLAINING THE PROCESS OF RENEWING THE MIND INTO THE CONSCIOUS EXPERIENCE OF THE KINGDOM REALM

The structure of all consciousness is information— patterns that materialize through the informations assembly. One cannot enter the realm of Kingdom consciousness until one seeks first the information of the Kingdom long enough for the information to be patterned in likeness to the reality contained in the Kingdom realm. The steady flow of information received while seeking first the Kingdom is the process that develops the renewed mind which is consciousness of the Kingdom. The blueprints for the infrastructure of the Kingdom are concealed in the renewed mind. In order to introduce the process of developing the renewed mind in greater detail, we must lay a foundation.

This foundation begins with the neuroscientific theory of changing our field of consciousness from this world system to the Kingdom. Understanding the integrated information theory of consciousness sheds light on why Jesus commanded us to seek first the Kingdom, and why He chose to come to earth as a teacher who gathered students. A disciple is a student of Jesus. When we transition from a follower to a disciple, we commit to receiving information of the Kingdom as we seek first the Kingdom. This activity alone is what will transform the mind into conscious experience of the Kingdom, practically placing you in the Kingdom on earth. To be transformed by the renewing of the mind is to be transported into the realm of the Kingdom through the appearing of the Kingdom field of consciousness subjectively.

Christof Koch is an American neuroscientist best known for his work on the neural basis of consciousness. He is the President and Chief Scientific Officer of the Allen Institute for Brain Science in Seattle. In a November 2013 Ted Talk, Christof said the following regarding neuron communities and their role in generating consciousness. This is not a quote, rather a rendering of his words as best I can. Christof explained that the integrated information theory of consciousness says, for any one system in a particular state, of which a brain is a particular system, the neurons are firing in one place but not in another. You can associate with this system, like a brain system, a number called the integrated number. It's measured in bits. It tells how integrated the system is. It's like synergy to the extent that the whole is greater than the union of its parts. The more integrated the system is, the more holistic it is. The more unitary it is, the more the system has integrated information. We are only conscious of states of our brain where the information is integrated from an assembly of parts into a whole. The moment the neuron assembly transitions into a whole, conscious experience emerges. Integrated information forms a precise representative neuronal community. The degree the information is integrated, denotes the magnitude of consciousness both in quality and quantity. The quality and quantity of consciousness in any one field is directly correlated to the information's amalgamation.

David Balduzzi and Giulio Tononi published a research article in 2009 entitled *Qualia: the Geometry of Integrated Information*. In it, they state,

"According to the integrated information theory, the quantity of consciousness is the amount of integrated information generated by a complex of elements, and the quality of experience is specified by the informational relationships it generates."

The key to conscious experience in the integrated information theory is the information developing into a specific pattern. A pattern that forms a whole is also called a maximally irreducible conceptual structure. Such a pattern is the end result of a sum total of parts which is the conscious experience. Patterns of the mind, when matched with patterns that exist outside of ourselves, form a conscious experience. When we conform to the patterns of the Kingdom, as opposed to conforming to the patterns of this world, we enter Kingdom consciousness. This transpires as we integrate Kingdom information by seeking first the Kingdom.

Each conscious experience requires its own independent neural network. These neural networks are formed through the integration of information. As we receive information within a particular field, neurons in the brain gather the information and begin connecting. At first, as the information is assembling, the communal formation is recognized as an assembly of parts and does not generate a conscious experience. As the community grows and develops in its formation, it reaches a point where it is patterned in such a way as to become irreducible. The parts form a whole and take on a different essence. What was once an assembly of parts, carrying no service to human consciousness, suddenly mutates into a whole. Out of the whole, emerges a conscious experience. Before we seek first the Kingdom, all conscious experience is patterned by information that is fragmented. It is void of the essence of the whole which is the Kingdom, therefore it generates conscious experience of another world. This world was patterned and expressed from the carnal mind. To renew our mind, we must pattern the mind with information of the whole. This can only take place as we seek first the Kingdom long enough for the neuron assembly of parts to form a whole.

In order for us not to be "conformed to the pattern of this world, we need the essence of our mind to change. The substance of our minds presently is made from the pattern of this world, which formed the carnal mind with integrated information of the parts. The carnal mind is limited to conscious experience within this world's system. The carnal mind blinds us from the world of the Kingdom. However, as we renew our minds with the information of the Kingdom, we form new patterns or *qualias*, whose essence is of the whole which is the Kingdom. Once the information of the Kingdom becomes integrated to the point it reaches "whole" status, your mind conforms to the pattern of the Kingdom. This results in conscious experience of the Kingdom. Once the patterns that make up the renewed mind become the predominant patterns of the mind, the field of Kingdom consciousness becomes our primary field of vision.

Our minds match patterns that exist outside ourselves. These patterns are formed by information that assembles in the neuron structures of the brain and become the physical substrates of consciousness. The external world exists. In order for a human to experience even one thing in the external world, a pattern must form. That pattern is the external thing experienced. The pattern is formed by information integrated into a whole. Every single object perceived must have a mirrored pattern in the mind. We do not perceive into the Kingdom realm of consciousness because we have lost the "key of knowledge" which is information of the whole—the Kingdom. The information of the Kingdom is the only field of information capable of patterning the mind to form conscious experience of the Kingdom. Conversely, all other information is responsible for forming the mind of conscious experience of another world, one not governed by Jesus.

There are two sources of information: 1) information of the parts and 2) information of the whole. Integrated information of the parts creates consciousness in this world system. Integrated information of the whole creates consciousness in the Kingdom. One source bears fruit from the Tree of the Knowledge of Good and Evil while the other's fruit is from the Tree of Life. In order to have conscious experience of the Kingdom, you must enter the Kingdom. In order to enter the Kingdom, you must be transformed by the renewing of your mind. The renewed mind is the pattern responsible for the conscious experience of the Kingdom, and its vehicle of transportation is seeking first the Kingdom.

Jesus told Nicodemus, "You must be born again to see the Kingdom." Being born again provides us with the eyes to see and enter the Kingdom, not the sight, nor the conscious experience of the Kingdom. Kingdom eyes must grow and develop into a lens that enables perception and sight. An infant is born legally blind. So are we born blind to the Kingdom realm of consciousness. A child's sight requires a process of growth in order to see. So does the child of God require a process of forming sight in and of the Kingdom.

This process is what Jesus called repentance—a change of mind. This change of mind comes about as we commit to a life of Jesus' highest priority for mankind: seeking first His Kingdom. This act and this act alone will satisfy the brains need to form conscious experience of the Kingdom, creating sight and entrance into the realm of Kingdom consciousness. If you want to enter the Kingdom, you must change your mind with the essence of the Kingdom which comes to pass only through a commitment to seeking first the information of the Kingdom.

A TESTIMONY OF CONSCIOUS EXPERIENCE OF THE KINGDOM

My wife and I were in Hawaii in 2015. We flew into the Big Island and drove to North Kona, a city about 45 minutes from the airport. After getting our rental car, we hit the road. The first twenty minutes we saw hundreds of large trees full of budding flowers. It was beautiful! We also saw flowering bushes lining the roads, fruit trees everywhere, and scenery that made our emotions dance! Suddenly, I heard the Lord say, "This entire city is a garden." I immediately went into the Kingdom realm of consciousness and remained there for a day and a half. The things I saw and heard led me to believe He was teaching and showing me His process of creating a New Earth with Heaven's influence, beginning with transporting us into the realm of the Kingdom through a change in our field of consciousness.

This new earth will spring forth as a result of a change of mind. This change of mind is what brings all who have been transformed by the renewing of the mind into the system responsible for ushering in the New Earth. That system is the Kingdom of Heaven on earth. The renewed mind will become the Tree of Life that grows the leaves responsible for the healing of the Nations (see Revelation 22:1-2).

Our first stop was a Bed and Breakfast 2000 feet above sea level overlooking the Pacific Ocean. When we arrived, the owner came to greet us and take us on a tour of the property. It was a five-acre organic farm with beautiful views. Because my wife told him of our passion for organic food while booking our stay, he was eager to show us around. When we got to the main plot of land used to grow fruits and vegetables, it was breathtaking. He began sharing with us the different varieties of trees, explaining the types of fruit. Occasionally he would pull a piece off for us to eat. They were ALL delicious. What shocked me was when he began pointing to all the trees that were only one year old. They were huge and bearing fruit! Some trunks were already four inches in diameter and ten feet tall. The branches were full of fruit and sagging under the excess weight. Astonished, I asked the owner how this was possible. His only response was, "The environment." Although I realized the tropical weather played a role, I knew there was more. Little did I know I was in for an experience of a lifetime.

After our tour of the farm, Sheila and I ventured down to the side of the home with the most picturesque view of the ocean. It was sunset, and I was preparing my camera when the Heaven's opened and I suddenly became aware of many things. Knowledge of how his farm was producing such large and luscious produce in such a short time, dropped into me. Immediately, another dimension opened, and I knew I was in a deeper Kingdom realm of consciousness. I began wondering if I was taken into a dimension that held the New Earth described in Revelation 21. "Was I taken into a realm or was a realm that presently exists opened to me?" I didn't go anywhere in a spatial sense. I remained present on earth but simply stepped into a higher dimension that is present and available to those inhabiting the earth. That dimension is the Kingdom of Heaven and is accessible through the renewed mind.

Because space/time is a dimension, and Heaven is an eternal dimension, it could be said that space/time is contained in the eternal, which makes it a part of the whole. Since the whole is greater than a part and carries different substance from the parts, we can conclude the dimension of Heaven is superior, in all ways, to space/time. A question arises: is Heaven accessible, and if so, how? Under the presupposition that Heaven is available to us now, how is Heaven available now? Rest assured Heaven is a dimension as accessible as the one humanity is presently aware of and living out of. However, we have been blinded through conditioning by the information of this world's system—fragmented information, which has grown the carnal mind, bringing consciousness of Satan's system of governance. A restructuring of the mind with the information of the Kingdom is the doorway to enlightenment and entrance into Heaven. The key is giving your mind over to seeking the Kingdom!

I was standing next to my wife looking down at the Pacific Ocean as the sun was setting. I looked at her because I wanted to say something, but when I looked, I was stunned. I could tell she was experiencing something extraordinary but was unaware her perception was in another realm. Her expression of the beauty she was experiencing was coming from a position in Heaven, not on earth. I never saw such extraordinary awareness of beauty coming from her. Her facial expressions and emotional response were very different.

When the substance of the whole is added to our awareness, our awareness takes on a new life. We see with new eyes as the essence of what appears in our conscious experience is altered. Substance once hidden in plain sight comes to life and what we once thought was beautiful is now overwhelmingly beautiful. What we once saw is now filled with a Divine substance that appears and transforms our field of consciousness. It was as if she was momentarily transported to Heaven with me. Only the transportation did not come by leaving a place in space but rather through the movement from one field of consciousness to another—from the field of consciousness of the carnal mind to the field of consciousness of the renewed mind.

Seeing this caused me to become speechless, and we continued in our state of awe and wonder. The purpose of this story is to relate a number of principles connected to establishing both personal and communal consciousness of Heaven on earth that the Lord revealed to me during this experience. The prerequisite for expressing Kingdom culture on earth God's way is entering the Kingdom. This entrance begins the moment we are born again but is experienced only as the field of Kingdom consciousness begins opening to us.

I pray the fruit produced from this book bears the resemblance of the dimension I was privileged to walk in for that day and a half. It is my hope that we will witness a generation walking in this field of consciousness where the physical realm and the realm of the Kingdom are one. It is my earnest prayer that we become that generation.

Be Transported by the Renewing of your Mind

The mind is what the brain generates, and the brain is structured with information. The renewed mind is the gateway to entering the realm of Kingdom consciousness. Seeking first the Kingdom is the source of the construction material used to build the renewed mind.

> *"Look! I have set before you today life and prosperity on the one hand, and death and disaster on the other."*
> Deuteronomy 30:15, NET

There are two worlds in front of us: 1) the carnal world sustained in our stream of consciousness by fruit taken in from the Tree of the Knowledge of Good and Evil; and 2) the Kingdom of Light brought into our stream of consciousness through the renewed mind which is formed from the information of the Tree of Life accessed while seeking first the Kingdom. Repentance is the process of transition from one realm of consciousness into another.

Repentance is not a religious word; it's something we do all day every day. Each time a high school student enters a new classroom, he is repenting. Every time we transition from one activity to another, we must engage in repentance. When Jesus declared, "Repent for the Kingdom of Heaven is at hand," He was presenting an opportunity to turn our thinking to the greatest idea mankind will ever be presented with. He was giving us an opportunity to enter a way of thinking that would structure the brain in such a way as to change the mind, resulting in awareness of Heaven on earth. This change of mind is not limited to change within the confines of the carnal mind which maintains consciousness within the realm of this world system. Jesus' change of mind results in the appearing of the Kingdom field of consciousness entering our personal experience. Repentance Jesus' way takes one out of an entire field of consciousness and transports one's consciousness into His realm of domain—the King's domain of Heaven on earth.

This world is the soul's prison. Repentance is the key to freedom—first individually, then culturally. Repentance is an act with such profound implications it was both John the Baptist's and Jesus' first words spoken publicly. In fact, I believe, after 400 years of silence between the Old and New Testaments, it was God's first public address announcement.

Repentance means a change of mind. Conventionally speaking, we refer to this change of mind as going from one care or interest to another, from one school of thought to another, or one way of thinking to another. Additionally, we look at repentance as a change in the way we think. We might say repentance is going from thinking negatively towards a person to positively or moving from an ungrateful thought to a grateful one. These are all good examples of repentance, but I would like to expand the definition. When the body of Christ takes on the added components of repentance, we will begin experiencing a new way of life that more closely lines up with the one God Almighty intended for us. This added component of repentance provides the mind with substance responsible for transporting us out of the field of consciousness of the carnal mind and into the field of consciousness of the Kingdom. As Dr. Michael Brown says, "Repentance is a revolution which rewrites all the rules for the game of life."

Repentance is more than a change in thinking; it's a change in the brain's biological construct—the physical representation of the mind—which enables new vision and awareness to be formed. Repentance, set in motion with information received while seeking first the Kingdom, changes our perceptual field of consciousness. When we seek first the Kingdom, the mind becomes patterned in such a way as to bring the appearance of the Kingdom field of consciousness to our personal experience. The transition from the realm of the carnal mind into the realm of the Kingdom is slow and subtle, but each glimpse into the new world, each appearance of the Kingdom in our field of consciousness, awakens a deeper drive to continue. There comes a point in our pursuit of seeking first the Kingdom that the field of Kingdom consciousness becomes our primary field through which we see and experience life. When this transpires, we are ready to learn to walk in the realm of the Kingdom!

Because the mind is consciousness, to change our mind is to change our conscious experience. When Jesus called us to repent, He was inviting us to change our minds from conscious experience of a world He did not participate in creating. This world is a world kept alive and in ruling control by the carnal mind. Changing our minds with information of the Kingdom is the process by which we enter the field of consciousness of the Kingdom and begin collapsing not only the world of the carnal mind but its ruling power. All information flowing from the field of Kingdomology provides the brain with the material responsible for generating conscious experience of the realm of the Kingdom on earth.

Consider this: we think about 60,000 thoughts a day. Ninety percent of those thoughts we rethink over and over which causes them to become programmed in our subconscious. This programming conforms the mind to a certain pattern which in turn wires our brain to see through the filter created by our conditioned and programmed thoughts. Our biology, neuro-circuitry, biological chemistry, hormonal expression, the genes we express as well as the reality we become aware of is all determined by both our conscious and sub-conscious thoughts. These thoughts feed the neurons in our brains that are responsible for assembling and creating the physical substrates of the mind which is consciousness. When we change the way we think, physical and chemical alterations take place. The only possible way for a human to see and experience the Kingdom on earth in a manner which the Lord intended is to change what we're thinking about to thoughts received while seeking first the Kingdom.

Unless we change the way we think by altering the substance within the flow of information taken in, we are stuck in the mire of this world's pattern, limited to the field of consciousness of a world which is far inferior to the one we were created for. However, to seek first the Kingdom is to change the information content such that patterns within the field of Kingdom consciousness grow, develop and begin expressing to us the world within the Kingdom. Jesus' command to "seek first the Kingdom" has greater implications and deeper outcomes than we could presently think or imagine!

The brain processes 400 billion bits of information every second, but we're only aware of about 2000. Because our minds are constructed with patterns that express the carnal realm, these 2000 bits of information have to do with three things and only three: 1) the body; 2) environment; and 3) time. All of our self-awareness is rooted in these three areas. Renewing the mind with "seeking first the Kingdom information," rewires the brain to process bits of information outside of ourselves, our environment, and time, all necessary requirements to both experiencing the Kingdom within and the field of Kingdom consciousness on earth. We cannot have conscious experience of the Kingdom without information of the Kingdom being processed and integrated by our brain. This is why the present Church has been limited to sprinkles of the parts of the Kingdom.

Transformation takes time, but culminates in the removal of the laws that govern us in our environment of time and space, and translates us in and under a new set of laws—the laws of the Kingdom. Consider the potential of Kingdom cultural expansion on earth by considering this. If 2000 out of 400 billion bits of information produces the consciousness and quality of existence and awareness we presently experience, then what in God's creation awaits those who tap into a fraction of the additional 399 plus billion bits of information, specifically Kingdom information? Lift the vision higher, Saints! The Kingdom consciousness revolution is upon us!

According to neurophysiology, when we begin processing new information, the brain begins developing two independent neural networks. These two networks create a new vision that is like taking a flashlight with a light that shines on the 2000 bits of information and moving it onto new bits of information. When this happens, we experience realization which the Bible calls revelation. This realization is conscious experience patterned in likeness to the information responsible for developing the neural networks. Once these networks are formed, they need to become firmly connected to one another, otherwise we lose the revelation. But if we revisit the information long enough, the connections become hard wired together, and we possess the revelation. It becomes part of us. The information that becomes part of us then moves to another part of the brain where it is stored and becomes the substance that makes up our identity. All throughout this process, as long as we are taking in the information of the Kingdom, our brains are forming connections that are bringing a new field of conscious experience—the Kingdom field of consciousness.

Change demands we move from one place to another. When Jesus said, "Repent for the Kingdom is at hand," He was inviting us to move from our current place into the Kingdom realm through a change of mind. Jesus cannot reestablish His Kingdom on earth until He establishes us in His field of Kingdom consciousness. He cannot establish us in His field of Kingdom consciousness until we seek first the Kingdom long enough for the Kingdoms information to conform us to the pattern of His world.

The process of becoming aware of something is called observation and involves an intentional focus. This act is a skill developed through conditioning. We use the frontal lobes of our brains to observe. What separates man from every other species on earth is the size of our frontal lobe in relation to the rest of the brain. In humans, the frontal lobe is about 40% of the entire brain. The next closest species is the ape at about 16%. For you dog and cat lovers, it's about 7% and 3.5% respectively. The frontal lobe decides on action and regulates behavior. It's the part of the brain used in creating, and considering possibilities. The adjective best used to describe the frontal lobe is "intent" or "purpose."

Science has discovered, the more we practice meditation, focus, and intentional observation, the more the frontal lobe is energized and awakened. If we can develop the skill of observation within the field of "seeking first the Kingdom," we will awaken realities in our conscious experience that lie within the Kingdom. Then we will be better equipped to fulfill the Great Commission.

Everything in existence and everything that will be was first conceived in the mind. Jesus' declaration to "seek first the Kingdom" was, amongst other things, an invitation to activate frontal lobe activity in the direction of His Will, the Kingdom. Keep in mind, Jesus put the responsibility on us to change our minds when He told us to "repent." In the same way that John the Baptist was a forerunner to Christ, so too is repentance a forerunner to the Kingdom realm expressing itself on earth.

Repentance is a change in conscious experience through the shifting of our states of consciousness. Because the mind is conscious experience, when Jesus proclaimed, "Repent," He was telling us to change our consciousness. Because there are only two fields of conscious experience, we can conclude the following: since Jesus lives in the Kingdom and we live in this world, Jesus is inviting us to "come up here" into His world of the Kingdom. We do this by changing our minds which is the action that moves us from conscious experience of this world into the Kingdom realm of consciousness. The change of mind Jesus has prepared for us takes the observer into the realm of Kingdom consciousness where the invisible becomes visible, and the impossible becomes possible.

Author's Note: The distinction between the two fields of consciousness should not be mistaken with the myriad of states of consciousness we experience moment by moment. There are two fields of consciousness; the realm of the carnal mind and the realm of the Kingdom—the kingdom of darkness and the Kingdom of light. A state of consciousness is a single, subjective, personal experience within a specific field of consciousness. These individual experiences are determined by the same measure that determines which field of consciousness appears to us. That measure is the essence of the information responsible for patterning the mind. When information of the parts integrates, it forms a pattern that generates a conscious experience from the carnal realm. However, when information of the whole integrates, it forms a pattern that generates a conscious experience from the realm of the Kingdom.

The moment we begin to give our brain new information, it begins rewiring itself according to the information it's being fed. God established this principle of producing after its kind and applies perfectly to the process of conscious experience

(Genesis 1:24-25). Information generates conscious experience in formation to the information. The degree that we are able to observe, focus on, take in, and learn Kingdom information, determines the quality and quantity of the change in conscious experience. Put another way, the level of seeking first Kingdom information is directly related to the measure of perceptual awareness we experience in and of the Kingdom. A word is a bit of information. The words that are taken in while seeking first the Kingdom carry the substance responsible for expressing the field of Kingdom consciousness.

A psychologist, for example, perceives vastly different subtleties of human behavior than the average person. Why? Because, through years of knowledge attainment within the field of human behavior, they opened that specific realm up to greater awareness and insight. They have, through the craft of "seeking first" the understanding of human behavior, effectively created vision otherwise invisible to those who didn't "seek first" knowledge of human behavior. The act of seeking first a field of study opens conscious experience within that specific field, effectively making the particular field their primary field of consciousness.

Moving from a carnal mind to a renewed mind takes patience, perseverance, and a willingness to set our affections on seeking first the Kingdom. The substance used to create the mind God designed for humanity is found in the activity of seeking first information of the Kingdom. The future will reveal that no greater field has impacted and influenced humanity than the field of Kingdomology. We are on the brink of the birthing of the field of Kingdomology. May the pioneers awaken with wisdom and fortitude to carve out this treasure trove awaiting discovery!

"Those who live according to the flesh have their minds set on what the flesh desires, but those who live in accordance with the Spirit have their minds set on what the Spirit

desires. The mind governed by the flesh is death, but the mind governed by the Spirit is life and peace. The mind governed by the flesh is hostile to God; it does not submit to God's law (the laws that govern the Kingdom), *nor can it do so. Those who are in the realm of the flesh cannot please God. You, however, you are not in the realm of the flesh but are in the realm of the Spirit, if indeed the Spirit of God lives in you."*

Romans 8:5-9a, NIV

We can't experience, let alone express the Kingdom without seeing the Kingdom. We can't see and experience the Kingdom without having knowledge of the Kingdom which grows the synaptic brain connections enabling us to see and experience the Kingdom. We can't have that without a teacher providing us with the information responsible for bringing the Kingdoms appearance. We also need to become willing students of a teacher teaching the Kingdom. This is why Jesus brought the message of the Kingdom, made Himself a teacher, and invited followers to become students (disciples) in order to change their minds.

Once they could see and experience the Kingdom, they too could then become conduit's through which the Lord could demonstrate it and duplicate Jesus' life-mission. The disciples only had one pathway into experiencing the Kingdom; changing their field of consciousness by allowing the information of the Kingdom to change their minds. This model laid out for us by our precious Lord, and His disciples is the model for transformation into the Kingdom, starting within our field of consciousness and moving out into the world.

The disciples' devotion to the information of the Kingdom presented to them by Jesus became the substance that changed their minds. As their conscious experience moved from this world system to the Kingdom, they experienced a very different life. Their words came alive with transformative power, out of their hands flowed great authority, and they experienced entire cities being transformed with the culture and influence of the Kingdom.

What appeared before their eyes and ears became more and more filled with substance emerging from the field of Kingdom consciousness. All this was a result of dedicating themselves as students to a very narrow school of thought—the school of Kingdomology. None of Jesus' followers entered the Kingdom and began expressing it like the disciples. They couldn't have. They did not receive the information necessary to change their consciousness from the carnal realm to the Kingdom realm. A follower of Jesus only becomes a disciple once they commit to Jesus' highest priority—seeking first the Kingdom.

The thoughts within our brain are released and create the chemicals that make us feel what we're thinking. So, if I'm thinking shameful thoughts, my brain is releasing signals telling my body to produce chemicals that make me feel shame, which in turn causes me to think shameful thoughts. On and on the pattern continues until the shame becomes part of my identity. The Holy Spirit knows this principle, therefore asks us, through the Apostle Paul:

*"Finally, brothers and sisters, whatever is true, whatever is noble, whatever is right, whatever is pure, whatever is lovely, whatever is admirable—if anything is excellent or praiseworthy—**THINK** about such things."*
Philippians 4:8

If we are to be transformed into Christ's image, we must pick up the discipline of taking every thought captive, thinking about what we're thinking about (2 Corinthians 10:5). The discipline of thinking about what you're thinking about provides the awareness necessary to change the way we think.

The highest expression of Kingdom life can only be realized and walked out by seeking first the Kingdom because the Kingdom is the whole. The only way to conceive the Kingdom is through the study of the Kingdom. As our brains make way for us to perceive the Kingdom, we are awakened to it. Through patience and perseverance, there comes a time when the Kingdom takes hold of us by making an appearance in our field of consciousness. It is at that time we begin entering into the lifestyle where we entrust the parts of the Kingdom to the sovereignty of the King, trusting He will provide the parts as we continue seeking the whole.

The disciples were given an opportunity to experience this Kingdom realm of living on earth when they were sent out on their first mission. They possessed the message of the Kingdom and were thrust into a position of fully relying on the Kingdom. Listen to how Jesus took away the "parts" of the Kingdom and gave them the whole. As you read, try to imagine Kingdom life as being completely reliant upon Jesus being the owner of everything and we being recipients of whatever He chooses to provide for us moment by moment.

"These twelve Jesus sent out with the following instructions: Do not go among the Gentiles or enter any town of the Samaritans. Go rather to the lost sheep of Israel. As you go, proclaim this message: 'The kingdom of heaven has come near.' Heal the sick, raise the dead, cleanse those who have leprosy, drive out demons. Freely you have received; freely give. Do not get any gold or silver or copper to take with you in your belts—no bag for the journey or extra shirt or sandals or a staff, for the worker, is worth his keep. Whatever town or village you enter, search there for some worthy person and stay at their house until you leave. As you enter the home, give it your greeting. If the home is deserving, let your peace rest on it; if it is not, let your peace return to you. If anyone will not welcome you or listen to your words, leave that home or town and shake the dust off your feet. Truly I tell you, it will be more bearable for Sodom and Gomorrah on the day of judgment than for that town. 'I am sending you out like sheep among wolves. Therefore be as shrewd as snakes and as innocent as doves. Be

on your guard; you will be handed over to the local councils and be flogged in the synagogues. On my account, you will be brought before governors and kings as witnesses to them and to the Gentiles. But when they arrest you, do not worry about what to say or how to say it. At that time you will be given what to say, for it will not be you speaking, but the Spirit of your Father speaking through you. Brother will betray brother to death, and a father his child; children will rebel against their parents and have them put to death. You will be hated by everyone because of me, but the one who stands firm to the end will be saved. When you are persecuted in one place, flee to another. Truly I tell you, you will not finish going through the towns of Israel before the Son of Man comes. The student is not above the teacher, nor a servant above his master. It is enough for students to be like their teachers and servants like their masters. If the head of the house has been called Beelzebub, how much more the members of his household!"

"So do not be afraid of them, for there is nothing concealed that will not be disclosed or hidden that will not be made known. What I tell you in the dark, speak in the daylight; what is whispered in your ear, proclaim from the roofs. Do not be afraid of those who kill the body but cannot kill the soul. Rather, be afraid of the One who can destroy both soul and body in hell. Are not two sparrows sold for a penny? Yet not one of them will fall to the ground outside your Father's care. And even the very hairs of your head are all numbered. So don't be afraid; you are worth more than many sparrows. "Whoever acknowledges me before others, I will also acknowledge before my Father in heaven. But whoever disowns me before others, I will disown before my Father in heaven. Do not suppose that I have come to bring peace to the earth. I did not come to bring peace, but a sword. For I have come to turn a man against his father, a daughter against her mother, a daughter-in-law against her mother-in-law—a man's enemies will be the members of his own household.

Anyone who loves their father or mother more than me is not worthy of me; anyone who loves their son or daughter more than me is not worthy of me. Whoever does not take up their cross and follow me is not worthy of me. Whoever finds their life will lose it, and whoever loses their life for my sake will find it. Anyone who welcomes you welcomes me, and anyone who welcomes me welcomes the one who sent me. Whoever welcomes a prophet as a prophet will receive a prophet's reward, and whoever welcomes a righteous person as a righteous person will receive a righteous person's reward. And if anyone gives even a cup of cold water to one of these little ones who is my disciple, truly I tell you, that person will certainly not lose their reward."

Matthew 10:5-42, NIV

Based on the way our brain is wired, we perceive reality. We don't see what's in front of us, we see what our minds have conditioned us to see. My wife is an expert in administering the Rorschach test. This psychological test identifies the subject's perception using a series of ten inkblot pictures. They are recorded and analyzed using psychological interpretations and complex algorithms. One characteristic revealed by using this test is the seemingly infinite perceptions the subjects express awareness of. It can be assumed with relative assurance that we can identify what an individual's thought life consists of by looking at the perceptions concluded throughout the test.

Based on the essence of the patterns which make up our mind, we perceive either the present world system maintained by the carnal mind or God's world system revealed by the renewed mind. Both worlds are present on earth. The essence of the patterns that match objects of the Kingdom of light is formed as we receive information of the whole which is the Kingdom's information.

The reason we have yet to enter the Kingdom in experience is because the essence of our minds are patterned with information of the flesh. The essence of this information formed the carnal mind which brought the realm of the kingdom of darkness— the fruit of the Tree of the Knowledge of Good and Evil— to our subjective experience. As long as the carnal mind is in operation, and the renewed mind is yet to be formed, Satan has legal precedence to keep us in the field of consciousness of the carnal mind. But thanks be to God through Jesus Christ! For He has made a way for us to break free from that realm and be transported into a realm governed by the Prince of Peace!

Leaving the Realm of the Carnal Mind

"Since you have taken off the old self with its practices, and have put on the new self, which is being renewed in knowledge in the image of its Creator."

Colossians 3:9, 10, BSB

Knowledge carries an image. Knowledge of the Kingdom renews the mind such that the information brings the appearance of images from the Kingdom realm of consciousness to our subjective experience. According to the Holy Spirit, through the Apostle Paul, the key to putting off the old self and putting on the new self is knowledge. However, this knowledge carries a specific nature in it. Its essence bears the image of God and has inherent power to transform us into His image and transport us into His field of Kingdom consciousness. This power "grows up" the new man into the image of our Creator while transporting us into the realm of His domain.

Notice where the renewing is coming from—"in knowledge"—specifically, the knowledge that originates from the image of its Creator. This knowledge carries a "whole" essence and transforms us into its likeness—Jesus the Son of God. By taking off the old self and putting on the new self, the inherent power of information becomes a primary instrument used by the Lord to conform us. This principle opens the door to understanding the inherent, transformational power of information. No wonder Jesus told us to make sure our highest priority was seeking first the Kingdom. The coming sons and daughters of God will be renewed and transformed with the information bearing the image of their Creator through the seeking first of the Kingdom.

Seeking first the Kingdom sets off a series of reactions in the body and mind that breaks present continuity to this world's system. Seeking first the Kingdom simultaneously creates fresh continuity rooted in the new information being taken in. Every moment we are seeking first the Kingdom we are both breaking down the pattern of the carnal mind and bringing together the material used to grow and develop the renewed mind. There is a form within information whose essence manifests the moment our brains' assembly of the information shifts from a system of parts to a whole system—from information of the carnal mind to information of the Kingdom. When information of the Kingdom reaches a whole state, the pattern it forms is conformed to the field of consciousness of the Kingdom. This brings an appearance to our subjective experience rooted in the field of consciousness called the Kingdom.

Science has learned we mold and shape our brain through the ideas we take in and hold onto. As we pursue and seek out specific ideas and hold the ideas in our brain, we begin leaving templates of those concepts neurologically in the tissues. Those templates then become the lens for new awareness. Learning, therefore, creates the template while memory sustains and maintains neurological connections necessary to create awareness and conscious experience of the form within the patterned information.

Put another way, when we seek first an idea, the frontal lobe empowers us to drown out external stimuli not associated with the idea we are seeking. During these moments, as we focus on the information, our brain is rewiring a pattern of connections that associate with the specific information. Because the

Kingdom is eternal and infinite, theoretically, we can seek first the Kingdom and enter into transformational states every day for the rest of our lives. Perhaps this is what the Holy Spirit was trying to communicate through Paul when he said:

"Do not conform to the pattern of this world, but be transformed by the renewing of your mind."
Romans 12:2, NIV

and

"We all, who with unveiled faces contemplate the Lord's glory, are being transformed into his image with ever-increasing glory."
2 Corinthians 3:18a, NIV

Every time we learn something new our brain changes. It makes up to 2600 new connections every time we are introduced to new thinking (Kandell, 2000). However, if we learn the information but don't revisit it, the connections begin to break apart. Let's use this scientific discovery as a template and lay it over Jesus' command to "seek first the Kingdom." The "seeking" is the intentional focus of gathering new information which produces the synaptic connections in likeness to what is being sought after. The "first" ensures the connections remain because you will be revisiting the information since it's your top priority. During the repetition period of learning, the synaptic nerve endings begin forming a relationship. The more they communicate, the more connected they become. The more connected they become, the more the information is realized and actualized.

Dr. Joe Dispenza calls this connecting the period of firing and wiring. The connections that fire together, wire together! This process is no different than any other healthy relationship in that the more we communicate, the more bonded we become. The Kingdom of Heaven is like an ideal marriage; we become joined as one and spend the rest of our lives realizing the life contained within the union. Our commitment to the relationship ensures steady, continual revelation.

Once we've established ourselves firmly enough in a particular subject, our brain creates what are called biological neural networks which are clusters of neurons that have been connected long enough to form a community of neurosynaptic connections. As our neurons begin to form networks, they become physical representations of something learned. In light of this incredible creativity by our Creator, consider God's petition to Abraham when He said:

> *"Look up at the sky and count the stars—if indeed you can count them." Then he said to him, "So shall your offspring be."*
> Genesis 15:5, NIV

Could God have been giving Abraham an opportunity to begin thinking in such a way as to begin growing neural pathway connections enabling Abraham to enter conscious experience of the very thing the Lord desired to do through Him? Was it even possible for God to do through Abraham what He destined for him, without first rewiring his brain by changing his thinking? Could it be that the principle in Amos 3:7 which states: *"The Lord does nothing without revealing his plan to his servants the prophets …"* has greater implications then we first understood?

Jesus, by commanding us to "seek first the Kingdom," set in motion a perpetual rewiring of the brain and chemical continuity toward things pertaining to the world He brought us and designed for us. The human body is circular in nature. What it takes in, it produces, and through conditioning takes back in and reproduces. This cycle goes on ad infinitum until repentance occurs. As we receive information of the Kingdom, we begin the process of transformation from this world's realities to Kingdom realities— from vision of this world to vision of the Kingdom. As a general principle, we can't see the Kingdom and then believe. Impossible! It takes belief (structured information) in order to see.

Author's Note: A key to hastening the belief that takes a person into visualizing the Kingdom is conscious experience of the Kingdom. Whenever we express an "effect" of the Kingdom, we open up our minds to receiving the "cause" which is the Kingdom. Natural expressions of the Kingdom, such as love, patience, and joy do not appear to have near the effect as the supernatural. However, once the Kingdom effect is expressed, we must be prepared to provide the observers with understanding. This becomes the key to leading humanity into the sheep pen of the Kingdom. How beautiful are the feet of those who bring the good news of the Kingdom!

In the movie *"What the Bleep Down the Rabbit Hole,"* Dr. Candace Pert and Dr. Joseph Dispenza tell a fascinating story that sheds light on how the human eye becomes aware of its surroundings. The principle guiding the story states, "We match patterns that already exist within ourselves through conditioning." These concepts condition our minds and wire our brains to such an extent that they become the lens through which reality is projected. The story is told that when Columbus landed in the Caribbean, none of the natives on the island were able to see the ships, even though they existed on the horizon. The reason they never saw the ships was because they had no neuron connections in their brains or no experience that the ships existed. The lack of brain patterns matching the ships kept them from experiencing what existed right before their eyes. They noticed ripples in the ocean but saw no ships and wondered what was causing the effects seen. These natives became aware of the effects of something but were unable to see the cause. They had no conditioning to form a wiring within their brain that would enable awareness of the cause, despite it being within their line of sight. Every day one of the natives went to the shore and looked, but saw nothing but the effects of the ship. Day after day the same results were seen. After a period of intense seeking, the ships appeared in his line of sight. Immediately he went and told the other natives that ships existed and were the cause of the ripple effects. He began describing in detail the ships makeup. Because everybody trusted and believed in him and because the information being received formed the neuronal correlates of consciousness of ships, once they got back to the shoreline, the other natives were able to become aware of the ships. This sheds profound insight into the importance of reprogramming and patterning our minds by rewiring our brains through the receiving of Kingdom information.

"Do not conform to the pattern of this world, but be transformed by the renewing of your mind."
Romans 12:2a, NIV

Author's Note: In Biblical times, awareness of the Kingdom was, in certain periods and especially in Old Testament times, commonplace. This is evidenced by the "normal" supernatural occurrences and lack of surprise by those experiencing them. The minds of those living back then still held patterns of the Kingdom that afforded them partial consciousness of the Kingdom realm. Perhaps the 400 years of silence between the Old and New Testament was a period when humanity lost touch with the supernatural expressions of the two kingdoms in a deeper manner. Judging by the response of the bystanders and followers of Jesus, it appears He may have, on a large scale, brought a reawakening of the realities of dimensions outside that which the carnal mind is conditioned to see. Although it only took one bit of information to reach Adam and Eve's mind before "death" entered them, it took much longer for the mind responsible for bringing Kingdom consciousness to collapse. During the centuries, Satan continued to erect the carnal mind and simultaneously collapse the Kingdom mind. Jesus, the second Adam, brought us the information responsible for transporting us back into the Kingdom realm of consciousness.

We must seek first the Kingdom, for in it, not the Kingdom but the seeking of the Kingdom, is God's means of reprogramming and repatterning our brains with Heaven's substance. The action of seeking first the Kingdom results in the appearance of the Kingdom field of consciousness as the brain is conformed to Heaven's patterns. The whole world presently lies in the grip of the evil one because he has successfully controlled the means by which systems within society condition the mind. Satan has formed patterns of the mind that present his realm of consciousness to our subjective experience. The construction material used to build his realm in our consciousness is information received from the Tree of the Knowledge of Good and Evil.

Additionally, Satan has limited the essence of the information to be that which grows, develops, and maintains the carnal mind. What is placed before us becomes the material used to condition us. The Devil knew if he could simply remove the only threat to his kingdom on earth, conforming the mind to God's Kingdom by seeking first the Kingdom, then he could blind the minds of everyone from the one reality that defeats him.

We are all pawns in the game of life. Depending on who we are allowing to condition us determines whose world we enter. Seeking first the Kingdom ensures conditioning from the Lord and progressive wakefulness to His Kingdom and in His Kingdom. All other roads lead to being used by Satan to maintain the appearance of his realm to humanities conscious experience.

"But small is the gate and narrow the road that leads to life, and only a few find it."

Matthew 7:14, NIV

That narrow road is the road of "seeking first the Kingdom." This is the only road that will lead to the Church's designed role of making students out of nations until the kingdoms of this world becomes the Kingdom of Christ! Seeking first the Kingdom is the only road that leads us into the realm of the "come up here." This is the state where we find a new identity and begin working with God on His terms, not ours.

If we become aware of what exists out of what has been conditioned in our minds, then in order to see the Kingdom we must begin to make it our top priority. The substance within what we prioritize becomes the essence of what appears in our subjective experience. We must receive more information of the Kingdom than anything in order for the Kingdom to appear in our conscious experience. Our priorities predicate and establish what is conditioned in our minds. This determines which of the two kingdoms dominate our field of conscious experience.

The greatest hindrance to seeking first the Kingdom is all the good fruit growing on the Tree of the Knowledge of Good and Evil. We must come to grips with this and ask the Lord to make available to us fruit from His Tree of Life. Once we taste and see fruit from the Tree of Life, we are provided with substance from the Kingdom realm. The more we eat from the Tree of Life, the more our minds are formed with the substance responsible for the appearing of the Kingdom realm in our subjective experience.

When information of the Kingdom has yet to pattern our mind, by default our awareness is rooted in Satan's kingdom. In most cases, the awareness resides in the subconscious or unconscious mind, and we are unaware of the world we are navigating. What we put in front of us creates the brain connections that produce awareness of what's in front of us. This sheds light on the scriptures which say:

"For as he thinketh in his heart, so is he."

Proverbs 23:7, KJV

and

"According to your faith let it be done to you."

Matthew 9:29, NIV

Since humanities fall in the Garden, there have been two worlds in front of us at all times: 1) the kingdom of darkness and 2) the Kingdom of Light. The patterns that make up our mind determine which world appears to us. May a generation arise whose minds are conformed to the patterns of Kingdom consciousness!

"Look! I have set before you today life and prosperity on the one hand, and death and disaster on the other."
Deuteronomy 30:15 NET

The book of Genesis illustrates and establishes this principle further. In chapter 30 we have the story where Jacob is working for Laban and wants to quit. He asks to leave, but Laban tells him he needs to stay longer and asks Jacob what he wants for payment. Jacob responds with a peculiar answer by telling Laban he will go through his entire flock of animals and remove all the spotted and speckled ones. Jacob tells Laban "Those will become my wages." Laban agrees and removes all the spotted and speckled animals, placing them three days journey from the rest of the flock. While tending to Laban's flock, Jacob builds a picture of spotted and speckled animals out of natural material and places it in front of the feeding trough. The picture was placed directly in front of the troughs, so the animals would see it every time they came to drink. When the flocks were in heat and came to drink, they mated in front of the picture. They conceived and gave birth to that which was placed before their minds continually, spotted and speckled animals. The information contained in the picture was used to condition their minds which gave birth to the pattern rewired in their brains. Jacob found a principle to producing desired outcome which he kept in motion throughout the remainder of his time working for Laban. The result? Jacob grew exceedingly prosperous and came to own large flocks of spotted and speckled animals. More than that, he discovered a principle: what is put in front of us is birthed out of us. Put another way, what we seek first we become aware of to the point that present reality collapses and a new reality is birthed.

This relates specifically to seeing and expressing the Kingdom on earth. Consider Jacob's relationship to his son Joseph, a man known as a dreamer, one who used his mind to think big. No doubt Jacob was the type of father that taught his sons well. Sprinkled throughout scripture, we see evidence Jacob loved his son (Genesis 37:3) and spoke into his life (Genesis 49:1-2). Joseph was also his favorite (Genesis 37:3). In the writings of the sacred texts of Judaism it is said, "Jacob raised all his sons in the fear of God, and taught them the ways of a pious life." In light of this evidence, what do you think the odds were that Jacob not only told Joseph the principle he discovered but taught him how to appropriate it? How important do you think this principle was to Joseph ending up in a position of influence second only to Pharaoh? No doubt Joseph went through some difficult times, but God ultimately established him with more influence than any human in the known kingdom at the time. Joseph's mindset, his way of thinking, played a huge role in his ability to establish Kingdom dominion on earth. In order for the King of Heaven to have influence on earth, He must first find men or women whose minds have been renewed with information of the Kingdom.

The importance of seeking first the Kingdom cannot be emphasized enough. We must decide today to make it our top priority. To the best of our ability, we need to focus and be intent on the single-eyed pursuit of the Kingdom. For therein, lying dormant within the act of seeking first the Kingdom, is the existence of an awareness of the Kingdom that will ultimately begin collapsing the kingdom of darkness and begin restoring the Kingdom of light to our field of consciousness.

As stated earlier, repentance means to change the mind. Look at this "mind changing" experience as it relates to the bits of information we are aware of. What if we were able to stop the flow of information as it relates to our body, environment, and time and replace it with bits of information relating outside of time—a different environment? What if there was a way to rewire the brain so that we begin seeing and experiencing things God created us to see and experience. What if there was a way to allow specific information to rewire the brain so that what we see is seen with a different set of eyes providing us with added substance within our experience? What if, right now in the present, there was an environment set before us, created by God, available for us to step into? What if we trusted Jesus, the Word of God, to lead us down the path that would help us to begin making "Kingdom connections" in our brain, resulting in awareness of the eternal environment of Heaven on earth? We are entering the days of restoration that will result in great transformation. This transformation begins with the mind. In order to see the Kingdom and experience lengthier periods in it, we must change our minds by changing the information we choose to receive.

We must separate ourselves from the things of this world. Whenever we engage in things outside of the Kingdom, we reinforce connections within our brain that sustain the kingdom of darkness' rule over our field of consciousness. Conversely, as we devote top priority to seeking things within the Kingdom, we begin the connective patterning and rewiring that ensures the emergence of Kingdom realities. The more we remain anchored in Kingdom information, the more time our brain has to develop Kingdom connections. The more Kingdom connections, the more Kingdom awareness; the more Kingdom awareness, the more Kingdom wakefulness. To awaken in the Kingdom field of consciousness is to enter the environment of Heaven on earth. This is the calling and destiny of a generation, a generation that will seek His mind by seeking first the Kingdom!

To illustrate what goes on in the brain when a person is engaged in an activity outside of seeking first the Kingdom, let's use watching a football game as an example. We turn on the TV, and for the next three hours we subject ourselves to millions of pieces of information that are in turn creating a response in our brain as it receives the information. These responses are creating neuron connections that in turn express what we become aware of. A general overview of those three hours shows we have spent 100% of that time involved in receiving information outside of information taken in while seeking first the Kingdom. We must conclude, therefore, that we just provided our brain with three hours of material used to reinforce our awareness of the things of this world, particularly things pertaining to the field of entertainment. Additionally, we have provided Satan and his kingdom with legal evidence to maintain his system of rulership on earth through the carnal mind.

Let's now look at a scenario that builds connections aiding in the awareness of the Kingdom field of consciousness. Suppose we sit down to read a book which provides us with information of the Kingdom. We've devoted the same three hours seeking the Kingdom, only this time there is a rewiring of Kingdom connections. Our established connections, rooted in this world, may become confused and agitated. Our emotions may even experience negative effects, a sort of "withdrawal" from the things of this world. We have begun a transformation from one world into another. All transformation has a rocky beginning but by devoting those three hours to seeking first the Kingdom, we have succeeded in the beginning stages of changing our minds. Changing our minds by changing the biological construct of our brains will, through perseverance and patience, bring about the appearance of the Kingdom field of consciousness to our personal experience.

Keep in mind, every time we commit to seeking the information of the Kingdom we are engaging in what Paul referred to as, "Casting down imaginations, and every high thing that exalteth itself against the knowledge of God ..." (2 Corinthians 10:5a, KJV). To cast down is to take down or disassemble. Therefore, every time we seek first the information of the Kingdom, we engage in the disassembling of the carnal mind, that which has exhalted itself against the information of the Kingdom—the knowledge of God.

"Come Out from Among Them and Be Ye Separate" (2 Corinthians 6:17a, KJV)

When I began seeking first the Kingdom, I saw no change in my life's experience. It was as if I simply added another topic to the many other subjects I was paying attention to. There came a time when visible change began. Revelation of the King and His Kingdom became more plentiful. I started seeing TV shows in another light. People's behavior and conversation seemed to change. It wasn't the people or TV that was changing. The new information I was receiving was producing new connections in my brain that were having an effect on my present patterned connections which formed my conscious experience. As my desire for the Kingdom intensified, my perception change sped up. I realized a pattern. The more time I spent seeking the Kingdom, the greater the perception change.

My view of this world changed as my view of the Kingdom emerged. The more the eyes of my understanding were enlightened to the Kingdom field of consciousness, the more my physical eyes were opened to the Kingdom realm. The more I experienced the Kingdom realm, the more I desired it. There came a point where I was caught, captured, and consumed by the Kingdom. I entered the field of the Kingdom, and since then, I've been overtaken by it.

Throwing off the things that so easily entangles us requires that we begin disassociating with such things that are outside of the Kingdom. The news, most entertainment, television programming, and much of our daily conversation (all things outside of seeking first the Kingdom) are hours spent creating and reinforcing connections within the brain that facilitate the awareness of this present world by keeping alive the carnal mind. To renew the mind back to its original design we must go back to the source which is the Kingdom of God. To go back to the source requires seeking first the Kingdom and the Kingdom alone.

A Lens Forms a Space-Time Image

We cannot apprehend the Kingdom by studying, seeking, or focusing on its parts any more than we can claim awareness of an automobile by identifying a wheel. The parts may serve as a foundation, but until we seek first the Kingdom long enough to be placed in the field of the Kingdom, we will not apprehend the Kingdom. Nor will the Kingdom seize us, without us choosing the Kingdom to be our primary pursuit.

The information discussed in this chapter reveals biological evidence that we must establish the framework for Kingdom connections. To begin forming neural networks in order to actualize and materialize the reality of the Kingdom through the renewed mind is the established framework. The only way for this to take place is for us to begin taking in Kingdom information. Once we begin taking in the information, we need to continue this process over and over. This is precisely what Jesus meant when He said, "Seek first." The Church has spent virtually all of its existence introducing and exchanging parts while claiming it to be the whole and the world has perceived us a laughing stock. The kingdom of this world will become the Kingdom of God's once His sons and daughters pick up the mantle of seeking first the Kingdom and become settled in this most important of Jesus' commands.

KINGDOM LAW

Kingdom law is the system of governing dictates that the country of Heaven recognizes. They are responsible for conditioning the actions of its citizens. Kingdom law is responsible for expressing and establishing the culture of Heaven on earth. Righteousness is the primary means through which Kingdom law is established (For those interested in understanding righteousness, I recommend reading Chapter Two in my book *Discovering the Kingdom; A guide to Seeking First the Kingdom* and, Richard Hays' book *Righteous at Last*).

Kingdom law is superior to all other systems of law, and when enforced, is binding by the citizen whose been granted authority to enforce such law. Kingdom law is enacted on earth, not by doing something, but by discovering something—our identity in Heaven on earth. As a citizen of Heaven, we have been clothed with the responsibility to allow Christ in us to express His countries laws on earth. Discovering our identity in Heaven is a key component to activating Heaven's laws on earth, ultimately laying the foundation for the expression and establishment of Kingdom culture. Kingdom law will only be enacted on earth through people who ascend into the Kingdom realm of consciousness. The groups who first discover their identity in the realm of the "come up here" will be the model God will use to transform nations. Jesus is awaiting the arrival of living stones in His domain, then He can begin building on earth His way.

Earth and its surrounding atmosphere is the only territory remaining where the laws of the Kingdom of Heaven are not governing. Once established in the Garden of Eden, man forfeited Kingdom law on earth. Since then, the laws that govern the realm of the carnal mind have been the governing influence upon the earth. God's plan has always been to find humans who will reestablish His laws back onto the earth to the degree that communities, cities, nations, and ultimately the earth become filled with the governing influence of Heaven.

This influence spreads to the degree the Lord finds sons and daughters equipped to represent His Kingdom law. This equipping takes place in the Kingdom realm on earth, providing those being equipped with identities that are formed and flow from the "come up here" realm. Put another way, these laborers are released once they enter the Kingdom realm of consciousness on earth and are trained and equipped from such a place. It's essential these laborers are trained and equipped in the Kingdom realm. Otherwise, they will fall short. When God leaves His realm to come work with us in our domain, He is limited. However, when we ascend into His realm we begin working with Him, and the results are very different than anything we have seen the past 1900 years. Kingdom law can only be executed from the Kingdom realm.

In order to step into our identity as a carrier of Kingdom law, empowered and equipped to re-present Heaven on earth, we must understand a key principle by which law is established. This understanding lays the necessary foundation for the Lord to begin equipping vessels through which He establishes His law on earth. The following shed's light upon this key principle and opens a door for the Lord to begin guiding us down the path that leads to the appearance of Kingdom law on earth.

In Genesis 1:26, when God said:

"Let Us make man in Our image, according to Our likeness; and let them have dominion ..."

He was establishing a law; only humans have legal authority on earth. The word "man" in Genesis 1:26 is the word human and is a grammatical construct meaning, "a dirt body with a spirit." A human, therefore, is a spirit in a body. This is who God chose to have rule and dominate the earth on His behalf (Any spirit without a body is illegal on the earth). Since God is Spirit, He has made Himself illegal on the earth except when He finds a human to cooperate with Him. Satan is also illegal and needs a human being's cooperation, willingly or unwillingly. Both God and Satan must find a human to work through. Humans were created to rule the earth. The question is whether God rules the earth with a human or Satan rules the earth with humans. Put another way, the realm of consciousness that fills a human mind with its information is given legal right to rule the individual with the laws that govern that particular realm.

Author's Note: Any spirit outside a body is illegal on earth. This ought to be an encouragement to us by providing us with a fearless faith to excommunicate any spirit illegally trespassing on earth. However, when we see a spirit from God, we can have confidence that spirit is not in the earth but in Heaven on earth. This subtle yet necessary distinction provides the spirit's from God legal access on earth. Because the spirit is in Heaven on earth, its presence with us who are on earth in Heaven is legal. Therefore, the only spirits with legal jurisdiction on earth are those in Heaven.

"The highest Heavens belong to the Lord, but the earth he has given to mankind."
Psalms 115:16, NIV

Throughout history God has been cooperating with man, doing what He can to establish His Will on earth. Jesus came to earth and modeled the means to cooperating with God and became our example. When God cooperates with man, He descends to our level, and the result is our present condition on earth. When man cooperates with God, the effects of the life of Jesus become the outcome and Kingdom law is enacted and upheld. In order to cooperate with God, we must ascend into the realm of come up here.

God needs a body to exercise His Will on earth. He needs that body to enter the Kingdom realm on earth before He begins working in the manner in which He intends (see John 8:23). As a representative of the Kingdom Church, I pray we begin cooperating with God and His plans rather than asking Him to cooperate with ours. In order for this to begin, we must ascend to the realm of the "come up here" so we can be shown the keys responsible for our cooperation with God. Renewing the mind by seeking first the Kingdom is the primary key of entrance into the realm of the Kingdom. Once we enter the Kingdom realm of consciousness, the Lord can begin preparing us to express and establish Kingdom law on earth. Jurisdiction is defined as the practical authority granted to administer justice within a defined field of responsibility. Practical authority to administer Kingdom law on earth is only granted in the Kingdom realm. Therefore, we must "come up here" before authority to enact Kingdom law is granted.

"Therefore the Lord himself will give you a sign: The virgin will conceive and give birth to a son, and will call him Immanuel."

Isaiah 7:14, NIV

God sent us "Immanuel" which means "God in a body." Immanuel allowed God to come to earth while protecting the integrity of His established Word to give dominion of earth to humans. Jesus became the second Adam and lived a life that brought not only the appearance of the Kingdom but its laws and governing culture. "God in a body" became the foundation for such a reformation.

"For it is God who works in you to will and to act in order to fulfill his good purpose."

Philippians 2:13, NIV

"For to us a child is born, to us, a son is given, and the government will be on his shoulders ... Of the increase of his government and peace, there will be no end ...."

Isaiah 9:6-7, NIV

The child was the body; the Son was the spirit. The body made the Son legal on earth. Jesus is the body; Christ is the Spirit. Jesus made Christ the Son legal on earth. Jesus did what He did on earth not because He was the Son of God (Matthew 14:33, Mark 3:11-12, Luke 22:66-70, John 5:24-27), but because He was the Son of Man (Matthew 9:1-8, Mark 10:42-45, Luke 21:24, John 6:61-63). It was Jesus' body that made Him legal to enact Kingdom law on earth. God gave humans legal authority to do business for Him on earth. This legal authority once enacted brings to life a higher law through which to govern the earth and its systems of rulership. This law flows from the Kingdom of Heaven and is authenticated as we make visible Heaven's authority on earth. In reading the passage below, pay close attention to whom God entrusts "the power to judge."

Jesus gave them this answer:

"... Very truly I tell you, the Son can do nothing by himself; he can do only what he sees his Father doing, because whatever the Father does the Son also does. For the Father loves the Son and shows him all he does. Yes, and he will show him even greater works than these, so that you will be amazed. For just as the Father raises the dead and gives them life, even so the Son gives life to whom he is pleased to give it. Moreover, the Father judges no one, but has entrusted all judgment to the Son, that all may honor the Son just as they honor the Father. Whoever does not honor the Son does not honor the Father, who sent him. "Very truly I tell you, whoever hears my word and believes him who sent me has eternal life and will not be judged but has crossed over from death to life. Very truly I tell you, a time is coming and has now come when the dead will

hear the voice of the Son of God and those who hear will live. For as the Father has life in himself, so he has granted the Son also to have life in himself. And he has given him authority to judge because he is the Son of Man."

John 5:19-27, NIV

Jesus identified where He received His authority to do miracles when He answered:

"for the Father judges no one, but has entrusted all judgment to the son."

John 5:22

The word "judge" means "to give rights." So the Father gives no rights on earth but has given that responsibility to the Son. Jesus concludes by saying the Father "has given authority to execute judgment {rights} also because He is the Son of man" (John 5:27). Jesus is saying I have authority not because I'm the Son of God (the Christ) but because I'm the Son of Man, a human with a body. In the same way, God needs us to use the authority He's entrusted to us as humans to exercise Kingdom law on earth on His behalf. When we do, God's culture and influence flows out of Heaven and is established on earth. As humans find themselves living in the Kingdom realm, the earth will soon begin witnessing Kingdom law once again filling its territory.

"Meanwhile, David and all the house of Israel were celebrating before the LORD with all kinds of instruments made of fir wood, and with lyres, harps, tambourines, castanets, and cymbals. But when they came to the threshing floor of Nacon, Uzzah reached out toward the ark of God and took hold of it, for the oxen nearly upset it. And the anger of the LORD burned against Uzzah, and God struck him down there for his irreverence, and he died there by the ark of God."

2 Samuel 6:5-7, NASB

Another Encounter in the Heavenlies

I was led into the spirit and saw that the self-appointed guardians of the key of knowledge—information of the Kingdom—were dead. I knew there would never again come a time when Kingdom information would be lost. I could see the Garden of Eden on earth once again. It was as an acorn whose oak tree sapling had just broken through. I was taken to see the growing oak tree and knew it to be a future sighting. I came back to this place where multitudes unnumbered were walking past the dead body which I knew represented the self-appointed guardians of God's knowledge. I noticed a group who were paying no attention to the dead man. I realized this group was in two places simultaneously, walking past the dead man and worshiping before the throne of God. A thought surfaced in my mind, "God raised us up with Christ and seated us with Him in the Heavenly places." I thought, "We were never created to be in one place. Life in the Kingdom is a discovery of our identity in multiple places at once!"

My attention turned back to the scene where I saw life sprouting from the earth like grass growing in a yard. I asked the one standing with me what the growth was and a heavy, weighty presence came over me. I heard an eruption of praise coming from the throne. At the same time, the Lord spoke, "The sprouting is My law, which has taken root in the earth and is now manifesting." When He said this, a bushel of seed appeared, and I heard a voice say, "Scatter, scatter, scatter." I asked, "Is this Kingdom law?" The voice responded, "No, this is the seed from which Kingdom law sprouts."

I was then given one of the seeds. On it was written Matthew 6:33. I knew this passage read, *"Seek first the Kingdom of God and His righteousness."* A voice spoke, "This bushel is for the second harvest. You have much seed left in the first bushel. Leave now and tell those carrying the first harvest seed to spread it everywhere, every time you open your mouth. Trust the seed and don't concern yourself where it lands. Only take this with you." Suddenly, a light flashed before me, and I asked the voice what it was. He responded, "It's not for you to know. Take the seed and do as I said." When He said this, I was aware he gave me two things; he put one on my lips and the other in my heart. I knew them to be "In love" and "seek first."

I was then taken to what looked like a construction site. As soon as I got there, I lost my sight. The Lord spoke, "This is My room. I am building My Church. Be about your responsibilities and leave the building to Me. Anyone that concerns themselves with this room is in danger of being disqualified."

Immediately, I was back in front of the throne worshiping. I could tell the temperature was getting hot and noticed heat coming from the body of the Saints. The Lord spoke, "The more Kingdom law is established, the more seed becomes harvested. The more seed that becomes harvested, the more building material I have. Seed equals harvest; harvest equals building material." Then I heard the Lord say, "You carry the seed and decide what to do with it. We work together to bring in the harvest, and I do the building." It was then I saw the numbers 212. I asked the Lord what it meant and found myself swept away to the throne.

There I was given what I knew to be eagle eyes and heard the Lord speak, "I hear your cry to be pure. I hear your cry to live with Me. I have shown you the way to a cleansed temple. I have shown you what must take place. Only seal up what I tell you. All else, bring into the light, only remind one another as often as needed to seek first the Kingdom. Those who have entered My Kingdom, seek first Righteousness, for to those seeking first the Kingdom has become their identity. Those that have been led to the study of My righteousness will be lifted to another dimension in My Kingdom." I asked, "What's the next level?" My body shook, and I heard, "Pursuit of only doing what you see Me doing." I was then transported before the throne with an intense feeling of soberness and peace.

Laying there, immersed in peace, I pondered what the next level was. I heard what sounded like the Lord say, "Here is where we will meet when it's time for you to learn about the next level in experience. Until then, first, scatter the seed of seeking first the Kingdom. Second, seek to understand My righteousness out of your seek first the Kingdom identity. Third, pursue only doing what you see Me doing. Leave the sprouting of Kingdom law to Me." There was an abrupt end, and I found myself being carried away in a refreshing wind.

As I was caught up in this wind, I realized it had carried me into a room and a door opened. I saw the Lord standing on a threshing floor. On it was millions of crucibles. I could see through them even though they were solid. In the crucible, I saw Satan and his evil spirits were the fire. Different groups of Saints were in the crucible. Each crucible represented the degree to which the Saint's embraced the fire as the Lords hand of testing and refining. They were paying no attention to the evil and had accepted Satan and his company, not as an enemy but as a tool used for purification. I knew this to be a very important room for establishing Kingdom law on earth. For no Saint could be used to establish law without the cleansing of fire. A deep cleansing is needed to become co-creators of Kingdom law on earth.

I began seeing multitudes of Saints not in the crucibles and became grieved. They refused to enter and were not being purified. A voice spoke, "Keep your eyes off everything but your assignment. Don't be distracted. Seek first the Kingdom of God and His righteousness. Pursue only doing what you see the Spirit doing. The King is in a season of sprouting His law. When you see the collapse of darkness over an area and His law manifesting, make sure it's not "emotionalism." If it is, ignore the hype, regroup, wait, and pray." Suddenly, I was back before the throne where I knew only those with clean hands, and pure hearts were.

Author's Note: I knew the Lord would use the "revivals" birthed out of selfish ambition and emotionalism, but it was important for those with eyes to see, not to get involved. Rather, those with discernment are to stay disciplined on the tasks mentioned above; seeking first the Kingdom, seeking first righteousness, and seeking only to do what we see the Spirit doing. I also knew there would be authentic expressions of Kingdom revival. When we see authentic expressions of Heaven on earth, let it be a sign we have Heaven's backing to cautiously and reverentially begin listening for Heaven's signal to "release" Kingdom law. Kingdom revival is also a signal to "over-emphasize" the need to seek first the Kingdom. We are to devote pulpit time to preaching and teaching the message of the Kingdom. As we do, signs and wonders will be evidenced as a tool to make visible the invisible Kingdom and bring greater authenticity to our message. The message needs to be esteemed above the miracles. "Do not marvel that you have power ..." (Luke 10:20 paraphrase).

After spending time before the throne, marinating in what just transpired, I realized I was eating. Every bite contained millions of living organisms filling my body with what I knew to be Kingdom energy. I became overly consumed with the feelings the energy was generating when I heard a voice call from the horizon, "You must not abandon your mission for pleasure. You are always before the throne. Don't let your body and soul be swept away with sensual desire. Don't let the Philistines, your flesh, take the Lord's presence for personal satisfaction and gain."

Suddenly, a mountain appeared, and the voice continued, "You must relentlessly seek first the Kingdom and His righteousness. As you can see, your life is not dead yet. Over the mountain is another bushel of seed. This seed contains Kingdom law which is sealed for an appointed time." I asked if I could see it and the voice replied, "You will in future time." "When?" I thought. "When the contents of the food from Heaven is digested and collapses what's left of your sensual and soulish desires." Fear gripped me as I realized, more than ever, I was a sinner in need of grace. I began crying and felt the touch of a hand. Peace enveloped me, and a voice whispered, "Fear not, I have set aside a drink for you." I looked and saw a tall glass. Written on it were the words KINGDOM LAW. I wanted to drink it but knew it was reserved for those whose carnal, fleshly nature was dead.

I asked the voice if I could take a drink and suddenly an aroma rose out of the glass. It was sweet smelling, like oil pressed out of many fruits, creating a blended smell. When the aroma touched my nostrils, I felt a substance filling my body. Joy began spreading within. I knew it was destroying sensual and carnal desires. I became overwhelmed and felt surrounded by love. More than that, I felt I was being held in love. I knew it was the Lord, having felt this before in previous Heavenly visits. I asked Him what was in the glass and He swept me away.

I was before His throne with a great multitude, only I felt different. I knew the aroma from the substance in the glass had done something. I felt a greater union with the Saints around the throne. I heard an eruption in the sound of a voice. I thought of Jesus' prayer in John 17 as the voice exclaimed, "This is the unity that all creation has been groaning and longing for." At the moment of my realization, the seed bag from the other side of the mountain appeared before me. I asked the Lord, "When can we begin sowing?" My heart began galloping, and I heard, "It's not for you to know the times or the seasons until I reveal them. My people are pushing and moving ahead of Me. Seek first My Kingdom and My righteousness only, and the few that have reached the level of "pursuing only what the Father is doing," encourage them.

All your declaring, and commanding, and binding and loosing is premature and being done outside My Kingdom realm. These fleshly actions are keeping My rain from falling on much of the Kingdom seed presently scattered. My way is narrow. The greater awareness of My Kingdom, the narrower the focus becomes." The Lord continued, "Keep your focus on only doing what you see Me doing." My head began hurting as I thought of all the work needing to be done. The pain went as quick as it came. I felt something I knew to be a pin size portion of the mind of Christ touch my skull. As thankfulness arose, I looked and saw an ocean with water dark blue in color and nature. Out of the water came substances I knew to be material contained in evaporation. Then a voice spoke, "This Ocean represents the mind of Christ. Kingdom law is producing an evaporation of the information contained therein. Immediately, I was back before the throne worshiping.

I knew the end of my time in this place was drawing near. I had a strong desire to get back to earth and tell as many as possible of all I had gleaned. The first person in mind was my spiritual father. I envisioned greeting him with a hug from Heaven when suddenly an eagle the size of a farmer's field flew above me. He circled around and dove towards the earth. As his eyes locked with mine, I saw what looked like an entire universe. Written on his forehead was "Kingdom law continued." I asked the Lord, "What was that?" He motioned to the ground, and I saw nothing. I looked up with shrugged shoulders as if to respond "I don't see anything," but before I could speak, the ground lifted and was suspended off the earth. Grass sprouted from the suspended ground. Coming down from the sky were millions upon millions of sheep. They had the wings of a dove, eyes of an eagle, and wool growing out from their skin. They landed on the grass and began eating. Once they started chewing, I heard a voice speak, "These are My Kingdom Saints grazing on Kingdom Law. Wait now and see what happens." I knew what the voice meant. I understood the principle, "what you eat you become." As soon as I thought that, the earth collapsed, but the grass remained, suspended above the earth. Then I remembered the grass was the fruit from the seed of seeking first the Kingdom.

The spirit of Wisdom came and rested on my mind and said, "Kingdom law will be used to collapse the kingdom of darkness, creating a new earth in Heaven and a new Heaven on earth." I wondered, "What portion of the earth just collapsed?" Suddenly, a pair of eyes and ears appeared and together said,

"America, America." My heart skipped a beat, and they continued, "America will become the greatest instrument for establishing Kingdom law of any."

Suddenly, I was swept away into a room with Nazi propaganda. It was dark, very dark. I trembled in fear and my heart began beating fast. A dove rested on my heart and said, "Be of good cheer, I have overcome the world. Behold I am alive forevermore. I will never leave you." My heart resumed normalcy, and the dove continued, "I have given you many truths in this room. Keep them and keep resolute in your message. Go now and make students of nations. Start with America."

My attention drifted to Germany, and I began to cry as desire for the Kingdoms expression on that territory overtook me. Emotions of sadness were quickly overshadowed with a soberness that got my attention. An invisible substance materialized and formed a single eye, and I heard the words, "Keep your focus on My Will for this hour. Know the times and seasons. The work I have for you has been prepared from the foundation of the world. Before you were created, I numbered your hairs and counted your breaths. I took careful thought of your steps and watched over them to perform through you. Let Me do what I do. You do what I say. Keep focused on learning to do only what you see the Father doing." After He spoke, something sweet entered my mouth, and I knew the Lord had departed. I was before the throne overjoyed and resting. Enveloped in peace, I remained overjoyed and in a heavenly state of rest.

Thoughts on Law

A legal fiction is a fact assumed or created by lawmakers that is used to apply and make real. Due to man's fallen nature, the kingdom of darkness created a legal fiction. A set of laws were put in motion holding up and maintaining the culture and influence of the kingdom of darkness. Until we enter the

Kingdom of Light through the renewing of our minds, we are subject to the laws of the kingdom of darkness. Presently, the Saints are unaware of the two legal grounds on which we may stand. It's not until the one collapses and the other enters our awareness, through conscious experience, that we begin to shift out from under the laws of darkness. There is one earth but two systems on the earth. One is held up through laws which bring conscious experience correlated to the system, while the other has laws which bring conscious experience correlated to it. The presentation of awareness flowing from the laws governing the system is what ensures the system remains in governance. We must learn to enter the Kingdom realm of consciousness in order to express and establish the laws responsible for the formation of the Kingdom's system of rulership—first in our personal lives, then upon the earth. Kingdom-dwellers, those whose field of consciousness is streamed from the Kingdom realm, become the conduits through which the Lord establishes His Kingdom on earth. Only those who have entered the Kingdom field of consciousness become the conduit's through which the Kings laws become rooted and grounded in a culture on the earth. Once this begins, Kingdom culture transcends Heaven onto the territory of earth and a space in time is filled with Heaven on earth.

A legal fiction is not the true self, created by God. Rather it is a false identity forged out of the carnal nature of man. It's enmity against God and must be done away with by exchanging the carnal mind with the renewed mind. We live out the life created from our mother's womb or the life created in the Father's heart. All laws subject to the carnal nature are inferior in every way to the laws which govern and influence the Kingdom dweller—those who discover their image created in the Father's heart. These laws bring into existence the true nature of the restored man living in the Kingdom on earth. The only way to begin seeing and expressing Kingdom law is to begin seeking first the Kingdom long enough for transformation to take place. Because the transformation is by the renewing of the mind, we must understand the importance of information, specifically the information which is received while entering the field of Kingdomology. We walk in this field, the field where the Treasure lies, every time we participate in seeking first the Kingdom of God. Sooner or later, we will begin having Kingdom sightings!

When Jesus and the disciples walked the earth, they carried with them Kingdom law as evidenced in all they did and said. What we do is a reflection of which laws we're subject to. What we do is evidence of the nature we've become aware of and a reflection of which kingdom we have our existence in. Kingdom law was expressed through the disciples because their commitment as students of Jesus made them seekers first of the Kingdom. This commitment transformed their minds, bringing awareness of a new set of laws governing an ancient territory—the Kingdom of Heaven on earth. This awareness became evident as a result of being transported into the Kingdom realm of consciousness by way of the renewed mind.

The only way to begin the journey into Kingdom law is to collapse the carnal mind by providing the brain with information about the Kingdom long enough for the renewed mind to express evidence of the Kingdom realm. This act alone makes room for Kingdom law to actualize and awaken. Laws are not something you strive to attain. They are a set of fixed principles that exist. Awareness actualizes or sets in motion the form and function within the law. Where we reside, the field of consciousness we live out of, determines which set of laws we are subject to. If we are in the Kingdom field of consciousness, we are under Heaven's laws. The more time we spend in the realm of the Kingdom the more we become conditioned by its laws. If we are not in the realm of the Kingdom, we are subject to the laws of darkness.

Because law is the system of rules that a particular country, community or individual recognizes, the government expects its citizens to abide by them. Law manages and controls the actions of its citizens. Law, therefore, is superior to man. We are subject to law. Law is not subject to us. Law shapes and constructs behavior within citizenry, not the other way around. A citizen, once they understand the laws that govern them, simply acts within the bounds of the law. Understanding carries us into the law, providing us the substance needed to enact a particular law. Understanding becomes the conduit for Kingdom law and the anointing, to be released.

Dr. R.T. Kendall, in his book *The Complete Guide to the Parables,* put it this way: "When you operate in the power of the Spirit, what you do comes easily. You don't have to worry about it, and you don't have to 'work it up.' There is no human effort or fatigue. Another word that would describe the anointing is understanding."

The most important principle to entering activity under Kingdom law is allowing the information of the Kingdom to form conscious experience within the field of Kingdom consciousness. This state of existence can only come to pass through a change of mind. Transformation through the renewed mind, by way of seeking first the Kingdom, is the pathway. In no other way can Kingdom law be formed in us and expressed through us. If we seek to understand Kingdom law without the renewed mind, we will receive information lacking substance of the Kingdom because our mind will receive the information in its "part form." Until information carries the substance of Heaven which alters the information's essence, we cannot inherit Kingdom law. The whole is not only superior to the sum of its parts, the whole carries an essence altogether different.

Consider the Kingdom of God within us. When His government takes up residency and is given freedom to act, the first effect is death to self. As He rises upon the throne of our hearts, He begins planting seeds of revelatory information that brings forth life from His Kingdom. We see evidence of such life in scripture. Every supernatural testimony in scripture from God's children is evidence of Kingdom law in action. These laws are all lying dormant in the Kingdom within us, waiting for the King's approval of the renewed mind in us in order to set His laws free through us.

These laws are superior, in every way, to the present laws set in motion by the system of rulership of this world. Seek first the Kingdom and trust the King to lead. Start a Bible study using Kingdom material. We need to devote ourselves to becoming students of the message of the Kingdom. Commit to teaching the Kingdom. Remember to create a mindset of seeking the whole, never the parts. Seek the Kingdom until the mind has been Kingdomized. Then we will have liberty, as the Spirit moves us, to seek the parts of the Kingdom. Pray for one another, dream and dwell on thoughts related to the Kingdom.

Keep in mind that the disciples were students of the message of the Kingdom before they were endowed with power to express the Kingdom. They received information of the Kingdom long enough for the information to morph into understanding, at which time they were transported into the Kingdom realm and eventually became endowed with Kingdom power. "For this reason, I have been born, to teach the Kingdom ..." (Luke 4:43, paraphrase). If Jesus was born to teach the Kingdom and we are his followers, then we must conclude that we were born to be students of His teaching. When He established our highest priority to be seeking the Kingdom, He was providing for us the pathway to entering our relationship with Him as student. Our greatest reward of studenthood is entrance into the Kingdom field of consciousness! The place where we become co-laborers with Christ in establishing, on earth, the laws that govern His eternal, everlasting Kingdom.

"Is anyone among you sick? Let them call the elders of the church to pray over them and anoint them with oil in the name of the Lord. And the prayer offered in faith will make the sick person well; the Lord will raise them up. If they have sinned, they will be forgiven."

James 5:14-15, NIV

A citizen in the Kingdom accepts this passage as a principle of law. He doesn't come to the sick person needing to drum up faith and strive to believe as his hands are placed on the sick. Nor does he come to activate the gift of healing by studying the part of the Kingdom called healing. This is another example of the two structures of law and how they are lived out. There was not one recorded instance where Jesus did not heal. Understanding Kingdom law from the place of Heaven provides us substance that brings the invisible Kingdom into existence. When we're in the Kingdom, and we receive a revelation of a particular part of the Kingdom, we must seek to understand the part within the context of the whole. The only way this is done is when our primary field of consciousness becomes the Kingdom. It's during the transition process that the King rises to His throne and awakens awareness of the gift, which in the Lord's time, activates the laws of His Kingdom. Much brokenness is necessary to become a Kingdom carrier of healing, but it is necessary and will prove to be one of the most effective tools in gathering the harvesters of souls in the coming years.

Author's Note: An additional point worth mentioning from the above passage regarding the Church, James makes a declarative statement that "the prayer offered in faith WILL make the sick person well." This is because when the sick call the elders of the Church to pray, the Church is in the Kingdom realm and therefore expresses Kingdom attributes, one of which yields healing. We know the Church in the New Testament is in the Kingdom realm because the Church mentioned in scripture is built by Jesus; the place where He resides is in the Kingdom realm. The present expression of the Church is rooted in the carnal realm which explains our feeble attempts and rare successes in healing the sick. When our field of consciousness ascends into the realm of the Kingdom, then the Lord will find for Himself living stones to continue building His Church in His domain. "Come up here ... and I will show you" (see Revelation 4:1).

The disciples were also under Kingdom law and effectively brought conscious experience of the Kingdom on earth. But even the King holds jurisdictional rights of His law within us, and will shut it down from time to time in order to keep us humble and reliant on Him, for the flesh is never completely dead until we enter the eternal Kingdom. That's why the Apostle Paul died daily, as we ought to. As the following scripture can teach us, when we think we have the answer, that is the time to humble ourselves. When we see the activation of the law of Kingdom healing, it's time to take our fasting to a new level. In the Kingdom, each new Heavenly expression requires us to set our intentions on greater humbleness.

"When they came to the other disciples, they saw a large crowd around them and the teachers of the law arguing with them. As soon as all the people saw Jesus, they were overwhelmed with wonder and ran to greet him. 'What are you arguing with them about?' he asked. A man in the crowd answered, 'Teacher, I brought you my son, who is possessed by a spirit that has robbed him of speech. Whenever it seizes him, it throws him to the ground. He foams at the mouth, gnashes his teeth and becomes rigid. I asked your disciples to drive out the spirit, but they could not.' 'You unbelieving generation,' Jesus replied, 'How long shall I stay with you? How long shall I put up with you? Bring the boy to me.' So they brought him. When the spirit saw Jesus, it immediately threw the boy into a convulsion. He fell to the ground and rolled around, foaming at the mouth. Jesus asked the boy's father, 'How long has he been like this?' 'From childhood,' he answered. It has often thrown him into fire or water to kill him. But if you can do anything, take pity on us and help us. If you can'?' said Jesus. 'Everything is possible for one who believes.' Immediately the boy's father exclaimed, 'I do believe; help me overcome my unbelief!' When Jesus saw that a crowd was running to the scene, he rebuked the impure spirit. 'You deaf and mute spirit,'

he said, 'I command you, come out of him and never enter him again.' The spirit shrieked, convulsed him violently and came out. The boy looked so much like a corpse that many said, 'He's dead.' But Jesus took him by the hand and lifted him to his feet, and he stood up. After Jesus had gone indoors, his disciples asked him privately, 'Why couldn't we drive it out?' He replied, 'This kind can come out only by prayer.'"

Mark 9:14-29, NIV

What might the effects be if the Kingdom of Heaven had a different set of laws? What if, under this world system maritime law ruled the seas, UCC ruled business, and civil law ruled man; but Kingdom law ruled those under Kingdom jurisdiction? What if the renewed mind opened to us the realm of Kingdom consciousness which began raining down upon us a new set of laws to enact upon the earth.

In order to put law in motion, one needs first to interpret it, then apply it. Societal interaction with law only comes about through this process. Most live life tossed within the boundaries of law, taking for granted its rights and privileges. Until now, Kingdom law has been lost. Suppressed by the carnal mind, Kingdom law has been kept from us as we've lived our existence in the carnal field of consciousness. However, with the emergence of Saints seeking first the Kingdom, an increase in understanding Kingdom law has begun. The effects are soon to follow.

When Jesus said He came to seek and save that which was lost, He was referring not to humanity, like the Church has traditionally understood, but the Kingdom. The primary evidence that Jesus found the Kingdom was the visible expressions He presented of the invisible Kingdom. He did this through the enforcement of the laws of Heaven appearing on earth. Moreover, He carried the authority to overshadow the existing laws with the Kingdom's rule. Just because the Kingdom laws are superior in every way to all other laws, does not ensure they will be implemented and enacted. The Kingdom and its laws have been present on the earth since God spoke, "Let there be Light" in Genesis 1:3, but they require a human with certain credentials in order for them to be enforced and enacted. The foundational credential is abiding in the "come up here" realm.

Law is a tool a country uses to create culture, trust, and boundaries. It is never a master, always a servant. This is important to keep in mind. There is a hook in power that has swept even the best away from God. The Lord will always oppose the proud and extend divine empowerment to the humble. We must embrace the cross and surrender to its influence daily. Trusting the Lord, knowing He is faithful to keep us in even the most trying of times. God can only use a human greatly after they have been hurt deeply.

A statement of fact is law. Kingdom law is activated when our statements of fact become law. We can say all we want, but until our words express their substance, they are insufficient and not the law of the land. Until what is bound on earth is bound in Heaven and what is loosed on earth is loosed in Heaven, we have fallen short of our calling and election.

The constitution of Heaven is filled with statements of fact waiting to be appropriated on earth. A key to activation is entrance into the Kingdom. We must live in the Kingdom field of consciousness, in order for Kingdom law to become the law of the land. Right now the Church is attempting to activate laws outside the Kingdom by seeking the part desired to activate. This may bring results, but not Heaven's way. We are living in the days where fruit is no longer acceptable until it becomes lasting fruit. The only authentic Kingdom law activated and established is one activated from within the Kingdom field of consciousness. When we seek a part of the Kingdom, we have yet to enter the Kingdom. Get in the Kingdom and trust God to enact Kingdom law and give gifts as He sees fit.

The concept of law carries many definitions. In order to frame this idea of law, we must look at several words. The first word-group we will touch on is instruction, direction, teaching, and precept law. These ideas require understanding. As Kingdom citizens, we must not only have a firm grasp on the heart of God, but we must come to know His mind. Kingdom law is understood as we understand the Kingdom and its nature. We must study the Kingdom to show ourselves approved, a workman that rightly divides the information of truth. When we do, there comes a point where our words become like the legal and accepted currency within a nation. Our currency begins usurping the counterfeit currency which has been in circulation. Back in Jesus' day, someone who studied to show themselves approved was someone who only put genuine money into circulation. The present laws which provide the parameters for culture to live and move and have their being have formed our conscious experience and conformed our thoughts and behavior to a counterfeit, temporal world. Seeking first the Kingdom, as a community, will establish the order necessary for the Lord to begin providing us the authority to begin enacting Kingdom law on earth as we transition from life in this world to life in the Kingdom realm.

"In him, we live and move and have our being."
Acts 17:28, NIV

Enacted law demands cause and effect. Depending on which laws we operate under, determines our effect. In the Kingdom, faith is a set of beliefs that makes visible what is invisible. The vision is experienced both in the eyes of our understanding, as we teach the message of the gospel of the Kingdom, and in the physical eye as we express the attributes of the Kingdom. This circular reasoning of the establishment of Kingdom law goes like this: we preach the Kingdom and express the Kingdom and we bring sight to the eyes of the hearers understanding and enable their physical eyes to see the invisible. This circular pattern is repeated ad infinitum until a nation becomes students of the pattern. This principle for the establishment of Kingdom law is the means through which the mind is conformed to the pattern of the Kingdom. This conforming brings about a transformation by the renewing of the mind. The transformation by the renewing of the mind transports us into the Kingdom realm of consciousness where we're awakened to the substance and life in the realm of the Kingdom.

The Kingdom's belief system makes visible the invisible. Kingdom law cannot be understood without knowing the effect the mind has on the territory of earth. In life, our thoughts create certain connections in the brain that in turn express the mind. This circular pattern eventually produces strong enough connections so they become imprinted in another part of the brain. Once this happens, that particular thought pattern produces what we call an identity. When we begin seeking first the Kingdom, we begin the process of rewiring our brain from an identity in this world to an identity in Heaven. Once Kingdom connections begin, we avail ourselves to conscious experience of the Kingdom on earth. As we settle into our new life in the Kingdom, we make ourselves available for the Lord to release Kingdom law through us. The more minds that become renewed the more Kingdom law is expressed. The more expressions of Kingdom law the more the Kingdom system of rulership occupies the territory of earth. This is a principle for the Kingdom Church, on behalf of Heaven, to take back residency of planet earth, one region at a time.

As God shares revelation with us, consider it an invitation to begin rewiring the brain with information of the Kingdom. Don't think we're ready to activate the revelation. The first principle of revelation is the need to pray it back to the Lord. We must go through a process of transformation in order to properly handle the revelation. Knowledge demands another step in the Kingdom for it to be transformed into understanding. All knowledge void of this step ends in pride. This process requires patience, dedication, determination, and fortitude. In the same way, gold can only be purified through refining by fire, so too does Kingdom knowledge need to be refined into the purity of understanding.

"The beginning of wisdom is this: Get wisdom. Though it cost all you have, get understanding."

Proverbs 4:7, NIV

God's Word Translation puts it this way:

"The beginning of wisdom is to acquire wisdom. Acquire understanding with all that you have."

When we pull the veil back, we realize there are only two sets of laws—God's and Satan's. God's laws come from His Kingdom and bear fruit from the Tree of Life. His laws govern the realm of the Kingdom on earth. We see examples of this throughout Jesus' life and the life of the disciples. Jesus carried the Kingdom within perfectly, and we see the results; everywhere He put His feet, Kingdom law was activated.

Satan's laws are the laws set forth by the governments of this world and serve Satan's purposes. These governments are part of his world system and are used to maintain humanities connection to the kingdom of the parts. The governments bear fruit from the Tree of the Knowledge of Good and Evil. Both kingdoms are alive on earth, and both offer themselves freely to mankind. The key to entrance into conscious experience of one or the other is determined by the information we take in which conforms us to one world or the other. The information of the parts provides the mind with the substance that forms the field of consciousness of the "parts kingdom." Information of the whole integrates and forms the Kingdom field of consciousness into your personal experience.

Jesus knew this and became upset with a group of people who were attempting to take away the "key of knowledge" which is information of the Kingdom. He went on to say, "You yourselves did not enter [the Kingdom], and you hindered those who are entering [the Kingdom]" (Luke 11:52). To remove the key of knowledge which is information of the Kingdom is to keep yourself from entering the realm of the Kingdom. Conversely, to receive

a consistent flow of the informatic
entering the field of consciousness
receive the information of the Kin
of consciousness will be upheld in

Jesus never entered Satan's w
remained within His world—the
the desert, Satan attempted to lur
but Jesus knew better. Choosir
Kingdom was a great victory for Jesus a...

There is great emphasis presently in the Church, to ᴜ......
Kingdom" into the different arms of earthly government and their
systems of rulership. Whether it's electing Christians into political
office to change a nation, striving to reach the highest positions
in the healthcare industry to change healthcare, or taking over
university curriculum "for Jesus," we must understand that we
never go into Satan's world except to present our world to those
ensnared. Our focus and attention is seeking first the Kingdom,
with the intent of entering the Kingdom realm of consciousness
and becoming established in Jesus' world, the Kingdom of Heaven.

Rather than entering Satan's system of rulership in hopes to
change it, Jesus brought us His system of rulership and presented
it. The presentation itself drew multitudes out of Satan's world
system. While on earth, if Jesus would have had it His way, He
would have developed so many disciples that they would have
altogether collapsed Satan's system of rulership on earth, resulting
in His Kingdom being fully established and upheld on earth.
One day, Jesus will declare, "The kingdoms of this world have
become Mine." Until then, He's waiting for you and me to lay the
foundation for Him to build this reality upon. That foundation
is entering the field of Kingdom consciousness through His
command to seek first the Kingdom. Seeking first the Kingdom
is the vehicle of transportation that lands us in the realm of the
come up here.

A 600,000-pound plane operates under the law of gravity
as long as it is traveling under 160 mph. Once it exceeds that

comes under a new set of laws empowering it to
ossible under the laws of gravity. The fruit of Jesus'
s the result of living under the laws of the Kingdom.
y lived His life in the Kingdom realm which brought
ion of His world to the inhabitants of the earth. He taught
ese laws and invited us to experience them in our life. It all
egins by making Jesus' top priority our top priority—seeking
first the Kingdom of God and His righteousness.

The Kingdom of Heaven is the only government that has righteous citizens. A righteous human is capable of functioning under Heaven's laws on earth, not because of his moral excellence but because of his position in relation to the government of Heaven. We must understand what the laws of Heaven are before we can operate under them. Furthermore, we must enter the field of consciousness of the Kingdom in order to appropriate its governing laws.

For example, in Heaven when we lay our hands on the sick they will recover. When Satan attacks us and we are in Heaven, we command him to leave, after we are certain the Lord is not using him to sift us like wheat or refine us like gold. If we have the clear to rebuke Satan and he doesn't leave, we petition our government by going boldly to the throne of grace. We present our request before the King and trust His verdict.

There are hundreds of Kingdom laws that give expression to Heaven's culture and social norms. Until we discover them and position ourselves for the Lord to express them through us, we will fall short in our mandate to provide those ensnared in Satan's system with a way out. Until we discover these Kingdom laws in the Kingdom realm of consciousness, people will be subject to the laws of this world system, limited in their efficacy as we attempt to enact them.

"For no one can pour "New wine into old wineskins. If they do, the skins will burst, the wine will spill, and the

wineskins will be ruined. Instead, they pour new wine into new wineskins, and both are preserved."
Matthew 9:17, BSB

We are no longer under the law of Moses; we are under the laws of Melchizedek, who is the King of Righteousness. Righteousness is the tool God uses to establish His rule on earth.

"Thy throne, O God, is for ever and ever: a scepter of righteousness is the scepter of thy kingdom."
Hebrews 1:8, KJV

We are not under the order of Aaron and Moses (Heb.5:5-6). The order of Aaron was the order of the carnal realm on earth. The order of Melchizedek is the order of Heaven on earth. Jesus satisfied the order of Heaven, thus becoming King of righteousness. He passed this on to all who are born again and has given us the opportunity to rule on earth in Heaven through righteousness. Repentance,—changing your mind with the information of the Kingdom—is the doorway into ruling influence, ruling influence on earth according to the order of Melchizedek.

We have become the righteousness of God in Christ (see 2 Corinthians 5:21). A huge obstacle to experiencing righteousness is overcoming self-consciousness. We have conditioned our minds to focus on "self." Therefore we have established patterns in the mind, which play our sin nature over and over. We must break this cycle by accepting the finished work of Christ deeply and clothing ourselves with His righteousness every day. This is done most effectively through two primary means:

1. **Spending quality time with the Lord**—giving Him our time and attention, in order that He might reveal His nature to us. He is forgiving, slow to anger, accepting, unconditionally loving, etc. As we become still before Him, we prepare

to encounter the heart of God which is encapsulated in unconditional love and acceptance. Doing so enables the Lord to begin revealing the divine nature in us which is Christ. The more we understand and experience Christ in us, the less self-conscious we are as the King rises and takes center stage in our consciousness.

2. **Seeking first the Kingdom of God and His righteousness.** One component of this commitment is studying what Christ has done on our behalf, particularly how He has given us His perfection. This gift has purified us once and for all, allowing the Father to see us only in light of the perfection of Christ. In effect, we have been placed in Christ. The Father no longer looks upon our imperfections. He sees only Christ's perfection in us. Conditioning our mind with this truth is an important step in the process of becoming His scepter of righteousness.

A country's laws influence society's way of thinking and acting. It is also a predictor of outcome. The laws governing our health care, for example, predict surgical outcomes with pinpoint accuracy. Healthcare experts in America know how many people will have successful surgery, how many will die, and so on. Our healthcare system laws make behavior and outcome predictable. In every area of law, we find behavior and outcome predictable.

Law also creates language, and language is another huge determinate of behavior. Benjamin Lee Whorf, one of the greatest linguists of all time, wrote an insightful book titled, *Language, Thought, and Reality*. In it he shows how language conditions thought and thought creates reality. Law is a major contributor of a culture's language.

When I was practicing holistic health, there were words I could not use. The FDA could fine and even imprison me for using words like "healed." This law effectively minimized the healings that took place merely on the principle of Whorf's findings. Similarly, in the past 1900 years, Satan has succeeded in keeping Kingdom language from humanity. This veil of ignorance has kept humanity from the reality of the Kingdom's existence on earth. The more we express Kingdom language, the more thought is given to the Kingdom. The more thought that's given to the Kingdom, the more expansive its reality becomes both in our individual conscious experience and the collective consciousness of communities, cities, and eventually entire nations.

The key to coming under the influence of Kingdom law begins by entering the Kingdom realm of consciousness. Seeking first the Kingdom of God and His righteousness is the foundation. Once we've become established in this, we begin walking through the threshold of transformation into Kingdom dwelling. Doing away with the carnal mind will activate the laws which govern the nature of the man living under Kingdom Law. Look at the chapter on the mind as the means to the collapse of this carnal mind. Beloved, believe me when I tell you, the initial step is as easy as changing the way you think from our present thought to thoughts birthed out of the pursuit of information received while seeking the Kingdom. By seeking first the Kingdom, we ensure a transformation from conscious experience of the present world system to Heaven. We effectively transform from being a caterpillar to flying like a butterfly. Let's make our home in the air. It's time to stop crawling! "Come up here!"

In the parable of the wise and foolish builder, we discover a principle for wise building. In Matthew 7:24 (NIV), Jesus says:

"Therefore everyone who hears these words of mine and puts them into practice is like a wise man who built his house on the rock."

In this verse, Jesus draws a parallel: those that hear His words and put them into practice are the same as a wise man that built his house on the rock. What is the building material? Words, specifically words of Jesus received. A word is a bit of information. Every time we receive information of the Kingdom, the words are put into practice in our brains through the formation of neuron correlates of the information. This building material becomes the house which builds the field of Kingdom consciousness in us. Hearing the words of Jesus—information of the Kingdom—is the same as building our house, the temple of God, upon the rock of revelation.

CONCLUSION

There is a generation arising that will enter the Kingdom realm of consciousness. This will be a generation known as seekers of the Kingdom—the overcomers that will rule and reign with Christ on planet earth. Their lives will be given over to the pursuit of the key of knowledge–the information of the Kingdom. As they do, the realm of the Kingdom will arise and become their primary field of consciousness. They will become the carriers of the Kingdom. The conduit's through which the Kingdom is expressed on earth.

Before a generation of Kingdom-dwellers are birthed, a group of pioneers needs to arise. These pioneers are alive today. Some have entered the realm of the Kingdom and are learning to live from a seated position in heavenly places, while others are just beginning the transformation by the renewing of their minds. No matter where we are on this journey, if we desire to become a partaker of the divine nature, we can. If we desire to enter the realm of Kingdom consciousness it's available to us. The Kingdom is an equal opportunity territory. All who come to the well of seeking first the Kingdom will be given the water of life which is held in the information of the Kingdom.

Today, commit to seek first the Kingdom. Find a friend or start a Bible study while you seek the Kingdom together. Add a class on seeking the Kingdom at church or school. Better yet, be the first to open a school of Kingdomology! Commit to becoming a leader in the greatest movement ever to sweep the earth. This is the movement that will transport us from the realm of the carnal mind into the realm of the Kingdom!

RECOMMENDED KINGDOM BOOKS

The key to entering the realm of Kingdom consciousness is renewing our minds with information of the Kingdom. Information of the Kingdom is whole information, all else is of the parts. Information of the whole is the key of knowledge responsible for forming the renewed mind which transforms consciousness by transporting us into the Kingdom realm of consciousness. I am presently working on a treatise that I hope will connect the science behind Kingdom consciousness and its relationship to information of the whole. Pray for me as I launch out into the deep and let down my nets for a catch.

The following is a list of books I've found over the years that carries, in a general sense, the information of the whole. I attribute my entrance into the realm of Kingdom consciousness largely to these books. I have read, re-read, studied, and re-studied their contents to the degree that I was participating in seeking first the Kingdom. The emerging field of Kingdomology, the study of the Kingdom—information of the whole—will prove to be the catalyst that launches a student of Kingdomology into the realm of the Kingdom experientially.

Make a decision today to seek first the information of the whole by seeking first the Kingdom! Never stop reading the Holy Scriptures, but keep in mind that, until our minds are renewed, the scriptures are not perceived through the lens God designed for us. "The letter kills but the Spirit gives life"(2 Corinthians 3:6b). The life of the Spirit is contained and reveled in and through the renewed mind.

- *Cosmic Initiative: Restoring the Kingdom, Igniting the Awakening* by Jack R Taylor
- *Discovering the Kingdom: A guide to seeking first the Kingdom* by Michael Gissibl
- *The Kingdom: The Emerging Rule of Christ Among Men: The Original Classic* by George Dana Boardman

- *The Unshakable Kingdom and the Unchanging Person* by E. Stanley Jones
- *Kingdom Principles: Preparing for Kingdom Experience and Expansion* by Myles Monroe
- *The Principle and Power of Kingdom Citizenship: Keys to Experiencing Heaven on Earth* by Myles Monroe
- *Rediscovering the Kingdom* by Myles Monroe
- *Righteous at Last* by Richard Hays

You will also find my YouTube channel useful in the development of the renewed mind. All teachings on my channel are for the purpose of engaging in "seeking first the Kingdom" material. The YouTube channel is Michael R. Gissibl.

About the Author

Michael Gissibl has been a successful business owner for over 20 years, carrying out God's word to him to "train, equip, and release" employees, resulting in many protégés also having successful businesses of their own. After experiencing a dramatic health transformation in 2009, Michael pursued a holistic health certification. Upon completion, he established a private practice to carry out God's word to him to "restore My Temple." Michael has helped countless people to improve the quality of their lives through the restoration of the body, mind, and soul. His most recent endeavor has resulted in the publication of this book, as well as several others in the works. As a 2005 graduate of the *Morning Star School of Ministry*, Michael has held numerous teaching and leadership positions, and has been involved in several nonprofit organizations. His passion for the Kingdom message is deeply rooted and far reaching. Presently Michael's main focus is to consult with churches on how to enter the Kingdom realm of consciousness and grow his itinerant speaking ministry. Preaching the gospel of the Kingdom is his deepest longing.

Michael is married to Sheila, a Psychologist who is Director and owner of a clinic in Waukesha, WI, as well as a Professor at Mount Mary University. He is blessed with four children and treasures the joys and challenges of watching them grow into adulthood. He enjoys active involvement in their sports careers, as well as their spiritual development. His passion for traveling God's great land is second only to pursuit of Kingdom awareness.

Michael's previous work, **Discovering the Kingdom,** is available at his website and on Amazon.com.

You can connect with Michael at his website:

www.discoveringthekingdom.org

or contact him at *kingdomwakefulness@gmail.com*